JKJC

NOV -- 2020

JKJC

 WOLVERINE

 WEASEL

 HUMMINGBIRD

 SPINNER DOLPHIN

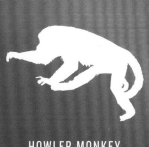 HOWLER MONKEY

PISTOL SHRIMP

CHAMELEON

CUTTLEFISH

 VAMPIRE BAT

 ASSASSIN BUG

ELEPHANT SEAL

 CUVIER'S BEAKED WHALE

DEATHSTALKER SCORPION

 BOX JELLY

 ORANGUTAN

CAMEL

BOWHEAD WHALE

 AMERICAN LOBSTER

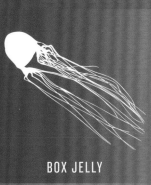 CANADA GOOSE

HONEYBEE

COCKROACH

 STRAWBERRY POISON DART FROG

GROUNDHOG

 NILE CROCODILE

 HAIRY FROGFISH

 MACARONI PENGUIN

 BROWN BEAR

 BENGAL TIGER

 CLOWNFISH AND ANEMONE

 MONGOOSE AND WARTHOG

ANIMAL SHOWDOWN

SURPRISING ANIMAL MATCHUPS
WITH SURPRISING RESULTS

★ROUND 3

STEPHANIE WARREN DRIMMER

NATIONAL GEOGRAPHIC
WASHINGTON, D.C.

CONTENTS

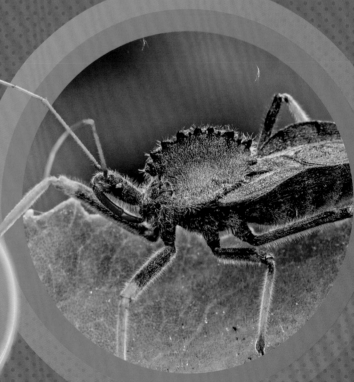

GRISLIEST GUZZLER

BEST HAIRDO

INTRODUCTION

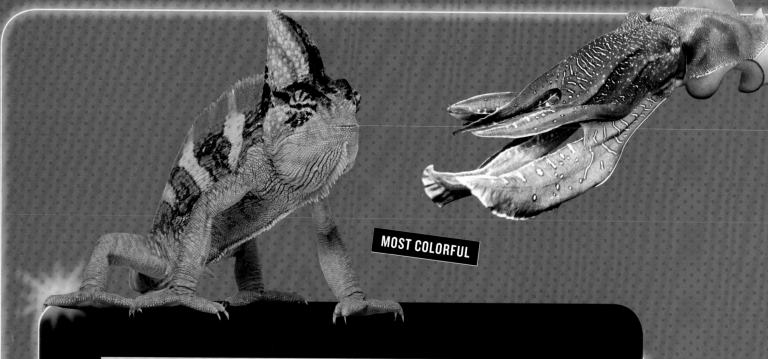

MOST COLORFUL

HAVE YOU EVER WONDERED WHICH OF EARTH'S CREATURES IS THE MOST VENOMOUS? WHAT ABOUT THE MOST COLORFUL, THE LOUDEST, OR THE MOST ACROBATIC? Get ready for some answers. In this book, chameleons face off against cuttlefish, hummingbirds challenge dolphins, and scorpions clash with jellyfish to find out who rules the animal kingdom. Along the way, the animals reveal all kinds of hidden talents and shocking secrets. Are you prepared for this battle of the beasts?

MOST VENOMOUS

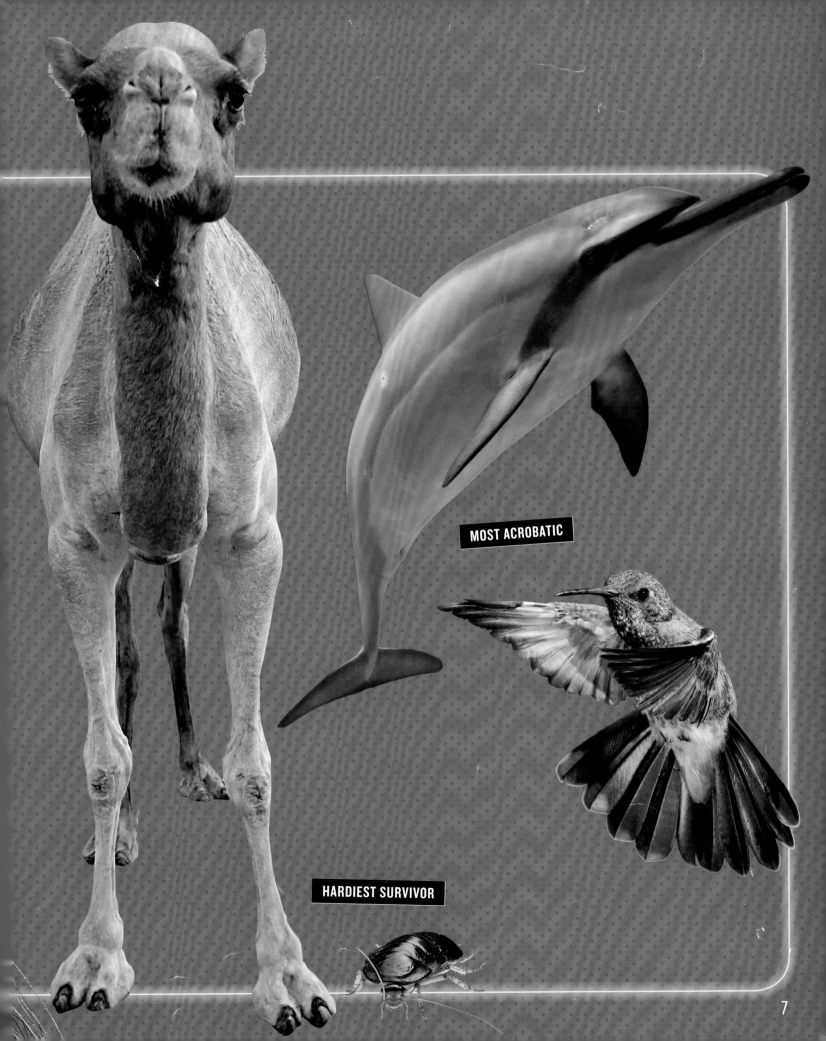

MOST ACROBATIC

HARDIEST SURVIVOR

FIERCEST

TALK ABOUT A BAD ATTITUDE.

These critters may look **CUTE AND CUDDLY**, but don't be fooled. They both have a reputation for going into **ATTACK MODE** at the slightest **PROVOCATION**.

WOLVERINE

> **THERE'S A REASON ONE OF THE X-MEN SUPERHEROES TAKES HIS NAME FROM THIS ANIMAL**—aside from the sharp, long claws the two have in common. Despite looking like a small, fuzzy bear, the wolverine is one of the toughest creatures on the planet.

Wolverines live in harsh northern climates where it's often cold and snowy. There, long winters mean food can be hard to come by. So when a wolverine gets a meal—often by stealing the leftovers from another animal's hunt—it will do just about anything to protect it. Wolverines are willing to fight with any creature that threatens to steal their food, no matter how big or ferocious.

WOLVERINE VS WEASEL

★ VS ★

WEASEL

> **WEASELS KILL LIKE JAGUARS DO:** by pouncing on their prey and then delivering death with a single, fatal bite to the back of the head. So it might be surprising that this predator is pint-size: Some species of weasel weigh just one ounce (28 g)—that's less than a golf ball!

Weasels may be small, but they can be vicious. They attack prey close to their own size, such as rats, but also take on more formidable foes: Weasels have been spotted going up against large birds such as herons. And one weasel species, the fisher, is so tough it's not afraid to dine on quill-covered porcupines. Talk about working for your meal!

We wouldn't want to catch either of these
ANIMALS IN A BAD MOOD.

WOLVERINES CAN **SMELL** PREY BURIED 20 FEET (6 M) UNDER **THE SNOW.**

WOLVERINE

COMMON NAME:	**WOLVERINE**	SCIENTIFIC NAME:	**GULO GULO**

SIZE:

20 TO **66**
POUNDS (9–30 KG)

WHERE THEY LIVE:

NORTHERN PARTS OF EUROPE, ASIA, AND
NORTH AMERICA

UNFRIEND ME
Wolverines are solitary creatures that travel great distances, roaming the frozen land alone. In 2009, scientists tracked one wolverine as it traveled solo more than 500 miles (805 km) through the United States, from Wyoming to Colorado.

MOST ANIMALS OF THE FRIGID NORTH CAN GO SEVERAL DAYS WITHOUT A MEAL. NOT THE WOLVERINE. Almost as soon as it's finished eating, it sets off in search of its next meal. **AS OMNIVORES, WOLVERINES CONSUME BOTH PLANTS AND MEAT.** But they don't stop there: They will eat just about anything—including bones and teeth!

DON'T BACK DOWN
Nothing upsets a wolverine more than another animal entering its territory or threatening to steal its meal. Wolverines will battle animals many times their size, from wolves to moose to even bears.

Weasels are always ready for a battle—and they owe their endless energy to their superpowered hearts, which beat up to 400 times per minute. **TO KEEP UP THAT EXTREME HEART RATE, WEASELS NEED TO EAT ONE-THIRD OF THEIR BODY WEIGHT EACH DAY.** That's like a 10-year-old chowing down on about 100 cheeseburgers every day!

STEALING HOME

Though weasels can easily dig their own burrows—where they spend the day sleeping—they often do not. Instead, they frequently take over the underground homes of other animals and claim them as their own. Hey, that's not very neighborly.

HUNGRY FOR MORE

Weasels are triggered to attack when they see movement, and they will still strike at prey even when their bellies are full. If they overdo it on a hunt, they will store their leftovers for later in underground "refrigerators" that they dig near their dens. One weasel refrigerator was found with 150 dead rodents inside. *Yum!*

WEASEL

WINNER

COMMON NAME:	WEASEL	SCIENTIFIC NAME:	GENUS MUSTELA

SIZE:

FROM ABOUT 1 OUNCE TO

12.3 OUNCES
(28–350 G)

WHERE THEY LIVE:

ALL OVER THE

WORLD

WEASELS HAVE BEEN SPOTTED KILLING PREY 10 TIMES THEIR SIZE.

Weasels and wolverines are not as well known for their hunting and fighting abilities as animals like lions or wolves. But maybe they should be. Both are bold enough to go after much bigger animals—and win! But which of them is the fiercest? Though they're the smaller of the two, weasels have one truly wicked habit: Before delivering their killer blow, they will hop back and forth in a "weasel war dance" meant to intimidate their prey. The dance has been known to paralyze rabbits with fear, causing them to freeze in place until the weasel inches close enough to attack. No contest: **WEASELS WIN.**

EXTREME-LY FEROCIOUS FIGHTERS

Most animals on Earth would rather **FLEE THAN FIGHT.**

NOT THESE CREATURES. IT'S BEST TO STAY ON THEIR GOOD SIDE.

CASSOWARY

This bird, which can weigh up to 167 pounds (76 kg), can't fly away from danger. So to fight off enemies, it strikes with the **5-INCH (13-CM)-LONG CLAW** it sports on one inner toe of each foot.

SUN BEAR

Sun bears may be the smallest bear species in the world, but that doesn't stop them from being dangerous. They're known to attack without warning, and their **SHARP TEETH** and **FOUR-INCH (10-CM) CLAWS** are vicious weapons.

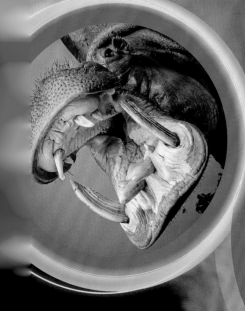

HIPPOPOTAMUS

Africa is home to all kinds of fearsome animals. But even predators like crocodiles and lions keep their distance from what is one of Earth's most aggressive animals: the hippo. **DESPITE THEIR BULKY, SLUGGISH APPEARANCE,** hippos are fast and agile and will attack wildebeest, buffalo, and even humans that get in their way.

FUNNEL-WEB SPIDER

Their venom is so deadly that it can **KILL A HUMAN IN 15 MINUTES.** And while these spiders don't seek out victims, they do have a habit of hiding in dark, concealed places—such as shoes. If disturbed, they will attack, using fangs so strong they can **PIERCE THROUGH FINGERNAILS.**

BULL SHARK

Bull sharks have a fearsome appetite. They **EAT ALMOST ANYTHING** they can find, including dolphins and other sharks. Though humans aren't normally on the menu, bull sharks frequent waters where people can be found, including coasts, bays, and even **FRESHWATER RIVERS.**

NORTHERN GOSHAWK

These agile birds are such powerful hunters that for more than **2,000 YEARS** they have been trained by people known as falconers to help humans hunt. They have **CRUSHINGLY STRONG TALONS** and don't hesitate to use them on any critter that comes too close to their nest.

MOST ACROBATIC

HIGH-FLYING FEATS: **HUMMINGBIRD**   WATER AEROBICS: **SPINNER DOLPHIN**

MOVE OVER TUMBLERS AND *TRAPEZE ARTISTS.*

Check out these amazing ANIMAL PERFORMERS.

HUMMINGBIRD

❯ *ZIP!* A BLUR OF GLITTERING FEATHERS WHIZZES BY. It's a hummingbird! These aerial acrobats are the stunt fliers of the animal world—able to soar at astounding speeds, make hairpin turns, and plunge into daredevil dives.

There are more than 300 species of hummingbirds, which live in the Western Hemisphere from Alaska, U.S.A., to Chile. The smallest is the tiny bee hummingbird of Cuba, which is about two inches (5 cm) long and weighs less than a penny. Hummingbirds use their small size to their advantage: They are extremely agile fliers. They can hover in place for long periods, and even fly backward and upside down—and they are the only birds that can achieve these feats!

SPINNER DOLPHIN

> **VISIT WARM OCEANS AROUND THE WORLD** and you might be treated to one of nature's most jaw-dropping performances: a pod of spinner dolphins leaping above the waves. Spinner dolphins travel in groups of thousands, and they love to show off their swimming skills.

Spinner dolphins get their name from the way they twist their bodies as they leap out of the sea. They can make several complete rotations before diving back into the ocean again. They often finish their "routine" with a flourish, slapping the surface of the water with their flippers or landing with a back or belly flop. *Splash!*

THESE ANIMALS HAVE SOME WILD MOVES!

But which stunt performer shines the most?

HUMMINGBIRDS GET THEIR NAME FROM THE HUMMING SOUND THEIR SUPERFAST **WINGBEATS** PRODUCE.

HUMMINGBIRD

COMMON NAME:	HUMMINGBIRD	SCIENTIFIC NAME:	FAMILY TROCHILIDAE

SIZE:

2 TO 8 INCHES (5–20 CM)

WHERE THEY LIVE:

NORTH, CENTRAL, AND **SOUTH AMERICA**

HIGH DIVE

Talk about some impressive moves! To attract potential mates, male Anna's hummingbirds fly high into the air and then hurtle toward the ground in showstopping dives. They can reach speeds of 50 miles an hour (80 km/h), or nearly 385 body lengths per second. In comparison, a fighter jet covers only 39 body lengths per second!

Hummingbirds can beat their wings incredibly fast— 70 TIMES PER SECOND IN NORMAL FLIGHT AND UP TO 200 TIMES PER SECOND WHILE DIVING. This allows them to attain speeds of **34 MILES AN HOUR (55 KM/H)—fast indeed for such a small bird!**

STUNT SECRETS

Most birds get lift, an upward force, from only the downward flap motion of their wings. But hummingbirds rotate their wing bones as they beat their wings, tracing a horizontal figure eight in the air. This produces lift on both the downward and upward flaps, allowing them to dive, hover, and fly backward.

SPINNER DOLPHIN

| COMMON NAME: | **SPINNER DOLPHIN** | SCIENTIFIC NAME: | **STENELLA LONGIROSTRIS** |

SIZE:

6.5 FEET LONG
(2 M)

WHERE THEY LIVE:

WARM OCEAN WATERS AROUND
THE WORLD

DO THE TWIST
These dolphins start their spin moves under the water, corkscrewing their bodies as they propel themselves toward the surface with their powerful tails. As they break free of the water, the speed of the spin increases, sending the dolphins twisting in as many as seven full rotations.

TAKE A RIDE
Spinner dolphins are often spotted leaping through the water in front of a moving boat—much to the delight of the humans onboard. The wave created by the front of the boat provides an effortless ride for the dolphins. *Whee!*

Experts aren't sure why spinners perform their signature leaps and twists. Perhaps it's to **ATTRACT MATES, SHAKE OFF PARASITES, OR COMMUNICATE** with the other dolphins in their pod. Or maybe these animals just like to **HAVE FUN!**

SPINNER DOLPHINS CAN LEAP OUT OF THE WATER **10 TIMES IN A ROW.**

There's no doubt about it: These animals put human acrobats to shame! But which has the coolest set of skills? While spinner dolphins deserve a round of applause for their leaping abilities, it's the hummingbirds that have the really heart-stopping moves. They can hover like a helicopter and dive like a fighter jet—actually, relative to their body size, they're faster than a fighter jet! Pretty impressive for a tiny bird many people can spot in their backyard gardens. **WINNER: HUMMINGBIRDS.**

EXTREME-LY GYMNASTIC ANIMALS

THEY *LEAP,* THEY *SPIN,* THEY WALK *UPSIDE DOWN!*

These creatures' **HIGH-FLYING FEATS** will leave you gasping in disbelief.

GECKO

⌃ With toe pads that sport about **A BILLION MICROSCOPIC HAIRS,** these reptiles use their superspecial feet to stick to smooth walls and even walk upside down on ceilings. This extreme cling power is possible thanks to the tiny toe hairs' electromagnetic attraction to whatever surface the gecko is on.

RED PANDA

⌄ These furry critters *have* to be acrobatic—they spend nearly their **ENTIRE LIVES IN TREES!** They climb high into the treetops to sunbathe. And when they want to come down, they can **ROTATE THEIR HIND ANKLES 180 DEGREES** to climb headfirst down the tree trunk.

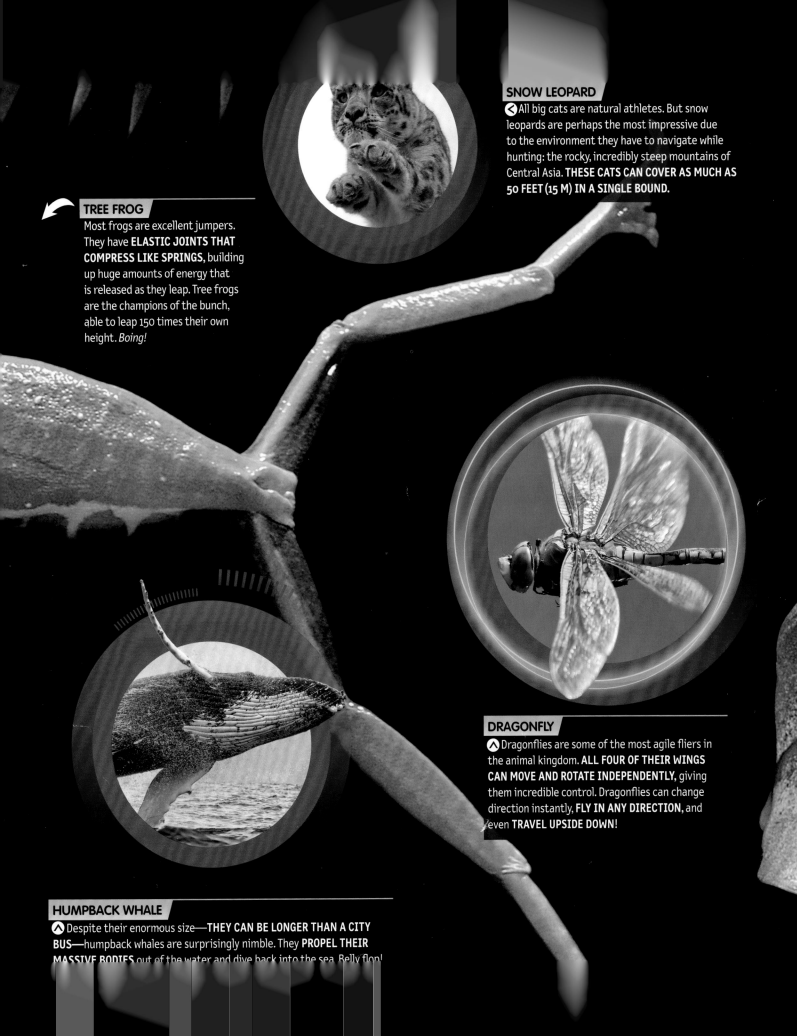

SNOW LEOPARD

All big cats are natural athletes. But snow leopards are perhaps the most impressive due to the environment they have to navigate while hunting: the rocky, incredibly steep mountains of Central Asia. **THESE CATS CAN COVER AS MUCH AS 50 FEET (15 M) IN A SINGLE BOUND.**

TREE FROG

Most frogs are excellent jumpers. They have **ELASTIC JOINTS THAT COMPRESS LIKE SPRINGS,** building up huge amounts of energy that is released as they leap. Tree frogs are the champions of the bunch, able to leap 150 times their own height. *Boing!*

DRAGONFLY

Dragonflies are some of the most agile fliers in the animal kingdom. **ALL FOUR OF THEIR WINGS CAN MOVE AND ROTATE INDEPENDENTLY,** giving them incredible control. Dragonflies can change direction instantly, **FLY IN ANY DIRECTION,** and even **TRAVEL UPSIDE DOWN!**

HUMPBACK WHALE

Despite their enormous size—**THEY CAN BE LONGER THAN A CITY BUS**—humpback whales are surprisingly nimble. They **PROPEL THEIR MASSIVE BODIES** out of the water and dive back into the sea. Belly flop!

LOUDEST

PLUG YOUR EARS!

What will happen when this **DEAFENING DUO** belts it out at **MAXIMUM VOLUME?**

HOWLER MONKEY

> **IT'S DAWN IN A SOUTH AMERICAN RAINFOREST,** and all is quiet. That is, until a spine-tingling noise fills the air. The booming cries sound like something uttered by some kind of terrible jungle monster. But they're actually the calls of a troop of howler monkeys.

Howler monkeys are the biggest monkeys in Central and South America. And they have a voice to match: Howlers are the loudest land animals in the Western Hemisphere. Each morning, male howlers greet the dawn with a high-volume performance. It says "Stay out of my way!" to other howler troops in the area.

PISTOL SHRIMP

> **THE UNDERSEA WORLD MAY SEEM CALM AND PEACEFUL.**
But duck below the surface and you'll realize that the ocean is one noisy place. Among the vocalizations of whales and the grunts and purrs of fish (that's right, some fish purr!), there's another sound— a constant clicking.

That's the sound of a pistol shrimp, one of the fiercest creatures in the sea. One of its claws is extremely oversize, and when the shrimp snaps it shut, it generates an intense burst of sound. Though these shrimp are rarely larger than your big toe, they can make a racket: In the tropics, the sound of their snapping is so loud that it's hard to hear anything else underwater!

HOWLER MONKEY
VS
PISTOL SHRIMP

THIS DIN IS DEAFENING! But who's the loudest of them all?

HOWLER MONKEYS **USE THEIR TAILS** LIKE A FIFTH ARM TO GRIP ONTO BRANCHES.

CRANK UP THE VOLUME

What's the secret behind the howler's earsplitting cries? Male howlers have an enlarged bone in their throats called the hyoid bone. Drawing air through a cavity in this bone amplifies their vocalizations, making the monkeys' calls incredibly loud.

Howler monkey calls **MEASURE IN AT UP TO 90 DECIBELS**— as loud as a power mower—and under certain conditions, they can be **HEARD MORE THAN THREE MILES (4.8 KM) AWAY!**

HOWLER MONKEY

CRY FOR PEACE

Howler monkeys might sound ferocious—but really, they're trying to avoid confrontation. Howlers would rather spend the day feeding instead of fighting. They howl to each other so that troops can stay spaced out in the forest, preventing mass monkey pileups at food sources.

COMMON NAME:	HOWLER MONKEY	SCIENTIFIC NAME:	GENUS ALOUATTA

SIZE:

BODY: 22 TO **36** INCHES (56-91 CM)

TAIL: 23 TO **36** INCHES (58-91 CM)

WHERE THEY LIVE:

TROPICAL REGIONS OF CENTRAL AND SOUTH **AMERICA**

PISTOL SHRIMP

COMMON NAME: PISTOL SHRIMP   **SCIENTIFIC NAME:** FAMILY ALPHEIDAE

SIZE:

1.2 to 2 INCHES
(3–5 CM) LONG

WHERE THEY LIVE:

MOSTLY TROPICAL AND TEMPERATE

WATERS

BUBBLE TROUBLE

The bang that the pistol shrimp makes doesn't come from its claws snapping together but from the bubbles that pop during that snapping motion. Besides producing a loud noise, the collapsing bubbles create a shock wave so powerful it can knock small prey out cold.

SOUND OFF

The sound created by the pistol shrimp is 210 decibels. That's louder than exploding fireworks, which can reach around 160 decibels.

The noise is so loud that it's been USED FOR MILITARY DEFENSE. No, really! Between 1944 and 1945, the U.S. Navy snuck submarines into Japanese harbors by navigating them among colonies of pistol shrimp. THE SUBMARINES' NOISES COULDN'T BE DETECTED OVER THE SOUNDS of the shrimps' bubbles.

TO GET SHRIMP TO SNAP TO MEASURE ITS VOLUME, SCIENTISTS **TICKLED THE ANIMALS** WITH PAINT-BRUSHES.

The howler monkey's call is one of the loudest sounds produced by any animal on Earth. And the pistol shrimp's snap is one of the loudest noises in the sea. So when it comes to volume, which critter reigns supreme? That title goes to the pistol shrimp: The collapsing bubble it produces is not only deafening and deadly, but it also briefly heats the surrounding water to 8000°F (4427°C)—nearly as hot as the sun's surface! **THAT EARNS THE SHRIMP'S SNAP EXTRA COOL POINTS, MAKING THIS CRUSTACEAN THE CHAMPION.**

EXTREME-LY DEAFENING CREATURES

WHAT? WE CAN'T HEAR YOU.

These animals are making too much NOISE!

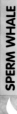

WATER BOATMAN

This tiny underwater insect is **SMALLER THAN A GRAIN OF RICE.** But it's the loudest animal on the planet, relative to body size. Its calls can reach **99.2 DECIBELS,** equivalent to the sound level you'd experience sitting in the front row at an orchestra concert. Even though 99 percent of the sound is lost when it travels from water to air, **THE WATER BOATMAN'S SONG IS SO LOUD THAT PEOPLE ON SHORE NOTICE IT.**

SPERM WHALE

These underwater giants **USE ECHOLOCATION TO NAVIGATE.** They produce clicks and then listen for the echoes to bounce off their surroundings in order to detect obstacles. Clicks clock in at more than 200 DECIBELS. In comparison, **THE SATURN V ROCKET ROARED INTO SPACE AT 204 DECIBELS**—and that was one of the **LOUDEST SOUNDS NASA HAS EVER RECORDED.**

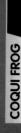

COQUI FROG

Ko keee ... ko keee. That's the sound of the coqui frog, named for its distinctive call. To attract mates, **MALES CHIRP AT 90 DECIBELS, ABOUT AS LOUD AS A GARBAGE DISPOSAL.** People in areas where there are lots of the frogs complain that these not-so-sweet songs keep them up all night.

BUSH CRICKET

> Male bush crickets scrape one of their wings along grooves on the other wing to **PRODUCE A SOUND AS LOUD AS A POWER SAW.** Thank goodness their songs are ultrasonic, meaning they're **TOO HIGH-PITCHED FOR HUMAN EARS TO DETECT.**

MOLE CRICKET

> This insect doesn't just sing—**IT BUILDS ITSELF AN INSTRUMENT!** The mole cricket uses its front legs to dig a burrow shaped like a megaphone, then stands inside the hollow to perform. **THE CRICKET CHIRPS AS LOUD AS A VACUUM CLEANER**—so loud it can be heard nearly 2,000 feet (600 m) away.

OILBIRD

> Like bats, **OILBIRDS USE ECHOLOCATION TO NAVIGATE WHILE FLYING THROUGH TOTAL DARKNESS.** But unlike a bat's calls, the oilbird's are within the range of human hearing. **THEY CAN REACH 100 DECIBELS, AS LOUD AS A JACKHAMMER.** When you consider that these South American birds roost together by the thousands, that's truly deafening!

LOVELY LIZARD: **CHAMELEON**   STYLISH SEA CREATURE: **CUTTLEFISH**

IMAGINE BEING ABLE TO CHANGE YOUR OUTFIT JUST BY THINKING ABOUT IT.

For these creatures, that **FASHION FEAT** is fact, not fiction:
They can transform the **COLORS OF THEIR SKIN IN AN INSTANT!**

CHAMELEON

> **A QUICK SCAN OF THE RAINFOREST FLOOR** might reveal nothing more than brown leaves. But look closer: Chameleons could be hiding in plain sight. These masters of disguise blend in perfectly with their background. But unlike other creatures that use camouflage, chameleons have a secret weapon: They can choose to stand out instead of blend in, transforming their skin into a rainbow of bright colors.

There are more than 150 species of chameleons, some as small as a thumbnail and others as big as a house cat. They live mostly in the rainforests and deserts of Africa. Their eyes can each move in a different direction at the same time, and their tongues, which they shoot out at top speed to snag prey, are about twice as long as their bodies. But changing their colors might be their coolest trick of all.

CUTTLEFISH

❯ SINCE THEY LIVE DEEP UNDER THE SEA, CUTTLEFISH ARE MYSTERIOUS CREATURES. There is still a lot scientists don't know about these animals and their relatives, squid and octopuses. And cuttlefish are certainly not as famous for their color-changing abilities as land-dwelling chameleons. But these up-and-comers are serious competitors for the title of most colorful.

At night, cuttlefish settle into the sand or hide in a reef, camouflaging themselves so perfectly that they almost disappear into the background. Then at dawn, they shake off their "nightwear" and blaze into a show of bright colors. As males battle rivals and woo females, they communicate by displaying incredible tints and hues. Their color changes are so sophisticated some experts think they could be considered a type of language.

CHAMELEON VS CUTTLEFISH

WHICH ANIMAL WINS THIS FACE-OFF of the most fashionable?

UNDER UV LIGHT, THE BONES OF SOME CHAMELEONS **GLOW** IN THE DARK.

CHAMELEON

COMMON NAME:	CHAMELEON	SCIENTIFIC NAME:	FAMILY CHAMAELEONIDAE

SIZE:

0.8 to 30 INCHES
(2-76 CM) LONG

WHERE THEY LIVE:

HABITATS

AFRICA, SPAIN, PORTUGAL, AND ASIA IN

RANGING FROM RAINFOREST TO DESERT

COLOR COMPETITION
When two males encounter each other, they duel for dominance in a pretty colorful way. They'll turn colors like yellow, red, or white, and even create a whole range of patterns. Eventually, the weaker male backs down—by "turning off" his display.

THE SECRET TO A CHAMELEON'S COLOR CHANGE IS A LAYER OF MICROSCOPIC CRYSTALS WITHIN THE REPTILE'S SKIN. THE CHAMELEON CAN CHANGE THE WAY THE CRYSTALS ARE SPACED, ALTERING THE COLOR OF LIGHT THEY REFLECT.

MOODY HUES
Like a mood ring, a chameleon can change its skin to reflect different emotions. These reptiles can darken their colors when they're frightened and brighten them when they're excited. Imagine if you could do the same!

COLOR SCIENCE

Cuttlefish have special cells in their skin filled with colored pigment. By squeezing muscles around these cells, they can stretch or shrink them to vary how much color is visible on their skin.

They don't just change their colors. They can also **CREATE INTRICATE PATTERNS,** such as spots or stripes on their skin. And they can even **CHANGE THEIR TEXTURE, RAISING OR LOWERING TINY BUMPS** to make themselves rough like coral or smooth like a stone.

SPEEDY SWAP

Cuttlefish can change the color of their entire bodies in a fraction of a second—about as long as it takes you to blink your eyes.

CUTTLEFISH

WINNER

COMMON NAME:	CUTTLEFISH	SCIENTIFIC NAME:	ORDER SEPIOIDEA

SIZE:

1 TO
35 INCHES
(2.5–89 CM)

WHERE THEY LIVE:

WARM, SHALLOW WATERS OFF WESTERN EUROPE,
AND AUSTRALIA,
AND IN THE MEDITERRANEAN SEA

A CUTTLEFISH CAN DISPLAY A DIFFERENT **PATTERN** ON EACH SIDE OF ITS BODY, COMMUNICATING TWO DIFFERENT MESSAGES AT ONCE.

Cuttlefish are sometimes called "the chameleons of the sea." They can not only change their colors and patterns, but also adjust their texture to blend in with what's around them. And while chameleons can't mimic just any background, cuttlefish can: In one experiment, scientists placed a black-and-white checkerboard in a cuttlefish tank—and these masters of disguise copied the pattern. **CUTTLEFISH FOR THE WIN!**

EXTREME-LY COLORFUL CRITTERS

MOTHER NATURE CAN'T RESIST A LITTLE FLASH.

Check out these **OVER-THE-TOP** animals.

CECROPIA CATERPILLAR

This bizarre beast appears to be covered with **SPIKE-TOPPED GUMDROPS**. And after the five-inch (13-cm)-long caterpillar crawls inside its cocoon at the end of summer, it emerges the following spring as an equally impressive adult: **A FUZZY, RED-STRIPED MOTH**.

RAINBOW BOA

< At first glance, this snake looks to be an ordinary shade of brown. But if the sun hits it just right, the **LIGHT REFLECTS OFF TINY RIDGES IN THE SNAKE'S SCALES**, lighting up the reptile in an impressive multicolored glow.

MANDARIN DUCK

< If animals had fashion shows, male mandarin ducks would rule the runway. These birds have **HOT PINK BILLS, PURPLE CHESTS, GOLDEN WINGS, AND CRESTS OF BLACK, TEAL, AND COPPER**. No wonder there was a stir when a lone mandarin—native to East Asia—showed up in New York City's Central Park in 2018.

MANDRILL

Mandrills might just be the **MOST COLORFUL MAMMAL ON EARTH.** Not only do males sport bright red-and-blue faces, but they have these **COLORS ON THEIR RUMPS** as well. Apparently, female mandrills find them irresistible.

FLAMINGO

Flamingos are famous for their bright pink color. But did you know **FLAMINGOS ARE NOT BORN PINK?** They get their **COLOR FROM A NATURAL DYE IN THEIR DIET OF BRINE SHRIMP AND ALGAE.** Since captive flamingos don't feed on these food sources, zoos once kept their birds pink by giving them carrots and red peppers. (Today, they use a synthetic supplement.)

PARROTFISH

The 80 or so species of parrotfish come in a variety of colors, from reds to greens to blues to yellows. And **THESE COLORS ARE OFTEN ARRANGED IN CRAZY PATTERNS.** Parrotfish also **ALTER THEIR COLOR OVER THE COURSE OF THEIR LIVES.** That has caused some confusion: Scientists first thought more than 300 species existed due to all the different-looking parrotfish swimming around!

GRISLIEST GUZZLER

REAL-LIFE DRACULA: **VAMPIRE BAT**   COLD-BLOODED KILLER: **ASSASSIN BUG**

YOU MIGHT WANT TO AVOID READING THIS BEFORE BED.

These animals are the stuff of NIGHTMARES!

VAMPIRE BAT

> **IN THE MIDDLE OF THE NIGHT,** when the sky is at its darkest, many of Earth's creatures are fast asleep. That's when vampire bats emerge. They pour out of the caves where they spend their days, gliding on nearly soundless wings. It's time for them to feast. And they only want one thing—blood!

Vampire bats are perfectly adapted to their bloodsucking lifestyle. They have an area in their brains that is specially devoted to detecting the regular, deep breathing of a sleeping animal. The bats land on the ground near their intended victim and hop closer. A heat sensor on their noses helps them locate a spot where blood flows close to the skin. They make a tiny, quick cut with razor-sharp teeth and then lap up the flowing blood with their tongues. Vampire bats prefer cows, sheep, and horses but have been known to dine on the occasional human. *Eeek!*

ASSASSIN BUG

❯ ONE TYPE OF ASSASSIN BUG IS NICKNAMED THE KISSING BUG. That sounds nice ... until you know where it comes from. These insects have a habit of biting people around their mouths and feeding on them. And what do they eat? Blood, of course.

There are more than 7,000 species of assassin bug. Not all of them slurp up blood, but they all have gruesome eating habits. Most use their pointed mouthparts, called rostrums, to stab through the outer exoskeletons of ants, termites, and bees. Then, they inject venom that paralyzes the target and liquefies its insides. When the ill-fated insect stops struggling, the assassin bug devours its victim's gooey innards. *Yikes!*

VAMPIRE BAT
VS
★ ★
ASSASSIN BUG

These **BLOODTHIRSTY BITERS** have us shaking in our boots.

FEMALE BATS WILL OFTEN **REGURGITATE**, OR **THROW UP**, BLOOD THEY'VE EATEN TO FEED NEW MOTHERS BUSY CARING FOR THEIR BABIES.

VAMPIRE BAT

COMMON NAME:	**VAMPIRE BAT**	SCIENTIFIC NAME:	**DESMODUS ROTUNDUS**

SIZE:

BODY
3.5 INCHES
(8.9 CM)

WINGSPAN
7 INCHES
(17.8 CM)

WHERE THEY LIVE:
THE TROPICS OF MEXICO,
CENTRAL
AMERICA, AND SOUTH AMERICA

PICKY EATER
Other bats can be found munching on all kinds of foods, from figs to fish to mosquitoes. Not vampire bats. They are the only mammal species on Earth to live on a diet of nothing but blood.

Vampire bats come **OUT OF THEIR CAVES WHEN THEIR VICTIMS ARE IN THE DEEPEST STAGE OF SLUMBER.** The bats are so lightweight and nimble that they can **DRINK BLOOD FROM AN ANIMAL FOR MORE THAN 30 MINUTES** without waking it up.

BIG APPETITE
In a single year, a colony of 100 vampire bats can drink the blood of 25 cows. Now consider that the bats can live in groups of more than 1,000. That's a lot of blood!

Assassin bugs have not just one but **TWO KINDS OF VENOM**. Besides the hunting venom used to take down prey, they have a **SECOND VENOM JUST FOR DEFENSE.** It has no effect on prey insects but causes **INTENSE PAIN IN BIGGER ANIMALS.**

HORRIFYING HUNTERS

Different species of assassin bugs use different strategies. Some will impale a dead termite and then dangle it into a termite mound until other termites come out to investigate. Others secrete sticky goo on their legs and use it to hold onto prey, turning themselves into a living sticky trap.

THAT'S HARSH

Some species of assassin bug aren't finished with their ant prey after sucking them dry. Once done eating, they stack the corpses of their spent victims on their backs, like a ghastly backpack. Scientists think they do this to protect themselves from their own predators, jumping spiders, which seem to detest the ants.

ASSASSIN BUG

WINNER

| COMMON NAME: | ASSASSIN BUG | SCIENTIFIC NAME: | FAMILY REDUVIIDAE |

SIZE:
0.2 TO
1.6 INCHES
(5–40 MM)

WHERE THEY LIVE:
MOST OF NORTH
AMERICA

ONE ASSASSIN BUG SPECIES STRUMS ON SPIDERWEBS TO MAKE SPIDERS THINK PREY HAS BEEN CAUGHT. THEN IT POUNCES WHEN THE SPIDERS APPROACH TO INVESTIGATE.

Yikes! These are two creatures we wouldn't want to cross paths with. But which one has the more shudder-worthy habits? Vampire bats certainly live up to their name, taking flight in the dark of night to feast on blood. But assassin bugs live up to theirs, too: They use all kinds of deadly weaponry and treacherous tricks to hunt and kill. And while bats leave their victims alive, assassin bugs don't stop at death: They actually *wear* the bodies of their past victims. **IN OUR BOOK, THAT MAKES THEM THE GRISLIEST GUZZLER.**

EXTREME-LY CREEPY CREATURES

THEY MAY SEEM MORE LIKE MOVIE MONSTERS THAN ACTUAL ANIMALS.

But here's the chilling truth: These critters are 100 PERCENT REAL.

VAMPIRE SQUID

They're named for their **DEEP-RED SKIN AND THE WEBBING BETWEEN THEIR FINS,** which makes the squid look like they're wearing a **VAMPIRE'S CLOAK.** Vampire squid are peaceful, shy creatures that live a half mile (0.8 km) below the ocean's surface. But when threatened, they flip their webbed arms over their bodies like an inside-out umbrella, **EXPOSING ROWS OF SCARY-LOOKING SPINES.**

AYE-AYE

It has wiry fur, huge ears, enormous amber eyes, and—oh no, what's that?—**A CROOKED, BONY, AND IMPOSSIBLY LONG MIDDLE FINGER.**

The aye-aye uses the dreadful digit to tap on tree trunks and **LISTENS FOR INSECTS** moving inside. Then it **CHEWS A HOLE IN THE TREE BARK AND USES THE FINGER TO SCOOP OUT THE BUGS.** *Shudder.*

VAMPIRE FINCH

⌄ **A BLOODSUCKING BIRD?** Believe it. This small finch, native to the Galápagos Islands, uses its sharp beak to **PECK AT BIGGER BIRDS UNTIL THEY BLEED,** then licks up the drops. How beastly!

FISHING SPIDER

⌄ **A SPIDER THAT EATS FISH** must surely be science fiction, right? Wrong. Fishing spiders are found on every continent except Antarctica. It hides at the water's edge until a fish comes close to the surface. Then—*WHAM!*—the spider attacks. **SUBDUING FISH THAT CAN BE MORE THAN TWICE ITS OWN SIZE.**

SHOCKING PINK DRAGON MILLIPEDE

⌄ What a **LOVELY SHADE OF PINK.** But this bug's bright color isn't a fashion statement. It's actually a warning to potential predators to keep their distance, because the millipede is seriously toxic. This critter produces **CYANIDE, A POISON SO STRONG THAT IN HIGH ENOUGH DOSES IT CAN KILL HUMANS IN MERE MINUTES.**

SARCASTIC FRINGEHEAD

⌄ To us, this creature doesn't look sarcastic; **IT LOOKS DOWNRIGHT SERIOUS.** The foot-long (30-cm) fish lives off North America's Pacific coast, where it spends most of its time looking like a normal fish. But if a predator gets too close, the fringehead **SNAPS ITS JAW OPEN TO EXPOSE ITS MONSTER-SIZE MOUTH.**

DEEPEST DIVER

HOLD YOUR BREATH — THESE ARE SOME OF THE DEEPEST DIVING ANIMALS ON EARTH.

But which is the **RECORD-SETTER?**

ELEPHANT SEAL

> **IN 2016, A MAN FROM NEW ZEALAND DOVE 335 FEET (102 M) DOWN INTO THE SEA—THAT'S NEARLY AS DEEP AS A FOOTBALL FIELD IS LONG.** It was the deepest dive made by any human in history unassisted by equipment. To do it, he had to hold his breath for four minutes and 14 seconds. For those of us who can barely make it to the bottom of the pool, this is a feat indeed.

But even the most impressive human athlete has nothing on an elephant seal. These underwater experts can plunge more than a mile—or 5,280 feet (1,609 m)—below the surface and stay down there for two hours at a time. They spend most of their lives at sea, performing their incredible dives to hunt. But when on shore, they're the marine equivalent of couch potatoes: They haul their huge bulk—males can weigh more than 4.5 tons (4.1 t)—on shore and loll around on the sand. Hey, all that

ELEPHANT SEAL
VS
CUVIER'S
BEAKED WHALE

CUVIER'S BEAKED WHALE

❯WITH ITS DISTINCTIVE FEATURES, IT'S HARD TO BELIEVE THIS MAMMAL COULD GO UNNOTICED. The Cuvier's beaked whale is about the size of a large car and has an indentation on its mouth that makes its head resemble a goose's beak. Still, these creatures are some of the most mysterious animals on Earth. Why? They are almost never spotted at the water's surface. Instead they spend most of their time below—deep below.

It wasn't until 2014 that scientists began to get a clear picture of how these unusual swimmers spend their lives. Scientists attached tracking tags to eight Cuvier's beaked whales off San Nicolas Island in Southern California, U.S.A. Then, they waited to see how deep the whales went. The answer shocked them: 9,816 feet (2,992 m). That's almost two miles (3 km)! Scientists know very little about how Cuvier's beaked whales accomplish this astounding feat. What they do know is that the whales are pushing the limits of what's possible.

WHEN ON LAND, ELEPHANT SEALS COOL DOWN BY USING THEIR **FLIPPERS** TO TOSS COOL SAND ONTO THEIR BODIES.

NO TANK NEEDED

Scuba divers carry air tanks on their backs. But an elephant seal's air supply is built in: They have so many oxygen-carrying red blood cells that their blood is thick and gooey. They also have extra oxygen-carrying molecules called myoglobin in their muscles. Weirdly, these molecules make their muscles black in color.

SEEING IN THE DARK

Very little light reaches the depths where elephant seals hunt. But that's no problem for these master divers: Their vision is 10 times more sensitive to light than a human's. Their eyes also adapt to the darkness of the deep sea much more quickly than ours: They need two to three minutes while we need 25 minutes.

ELEPHANT SEALS SWIM IN WATERS THAT CAN DROP BELOW 40°F (4.5°C). *Brrr!* Luckily, they sport an all-natural jacket: a **THICK LAYER OF FAT CALLED BLUBBER** that keeps them warm. An adult male elephant seal can be **50 PERCENT BLUBBER!**

ELEPHANT SEAL

COMMON NAME: ELEPHANT SEAL	SCIENTIFIC NAME: GENUS MIROUNGA

SIZE:

UP TO

20 FEET
(6 M) LONG

WHERE THEY LIVE:

NORTHERN ELEPHANT SEALS: **NORTH AMERICA'S PACIFIC COAST**	SOUTHERN ELEPHANT SEALS: **ANTARCTIC & SUB-ANTARCTIC WATERS**

At 3,280 feet (1,000 m), the WHALES ARE SQUEEZED BY PRESSURE 100 TIMES GREATER THAN THAT AT THE SURFACE. That kind of pressure is enough to compress air in their bodies, collapsing their lungs and causing permanent damage. To combat this, the WHALES CAN FOLD DOWN THEIR RIB CAGES to shrink air pockets.

DEEP-SEA MEAL

In the deep ocean, there is no light, almost no oxygen, and crushing pressure. Why would a Cuvier's beaked whale venture down there? There's only one reason: food. Scientists think the whales plunge to these depths in search of squid, which live in the deep sea in huge numbers.

AIR SUPPLY

You might take a deep breath before you make a dive. But not a Cuvier's beaked whale. Because lungfuls of air would make them float, these animals breathe out before they plunge, exhaling 90 percent of their oxygen. They use minimal oxygen during the dive by lowering their heart rate and shutting down body systems such as digestion.

CUVIER'S BEAKED WHALE

| COMMON NAME: | CUVIER'S BEAKED WHALE | SCIENTIFIC NAME: | ZIPHIUS CAVIROSTRIS |

SIZE:

15 to 23 FEET
(4.6–7 M)

WHERE THEY LIVE:

NEARLY ALL THE WORLD'S
OCEANS

TO CONSERVE OXYGEN, THE WHALES **SHUT DOWN** THEIR LIVERS AND KIDNEYS AND STOP **DIGESTION** WHILE DIVING.

Marine animal experts say that based on what we know, it shouldn't be possible for animals to dive to these extreme depths. How these creatures survive the cold, lack of light, and intense pressure is a feat so tough we are just beginning to understand it. Both these animals are incredible divers—but when it comes to which is better, there's no contest. Cuvier's beaked whales can dive down nearly two miles (3 km)—almost twice as far as elephant seals. **THAT'S LIKE PLUNGING THE EQUIVALENT OF EIGHT EMPIRE STATE BUILDINGS STACKED ON TOP OF EACH OTHER. WINNER: WHALES.**

WATCH OUT! THESE ANIMALS PACK A TOXIC PUNCH.

Read on to get the lowdown on these LETHAL CREATURES.

DEATHSTALKER SCORPION

> **THE NAME SAYS IT ALL.** The deathstalker scorpion is a stealthy hunter, remaining perfectly motionless as it hides under a rock waiting for a cricket or other unsuspecting insect to come along. Then, the scorpion springs from its hiding place, grabs the critter in its pincers, and delivers its deadly sting.

Deathstalkers have some of the strongest venom of any scorpion on Earth. This venom paralyzes or kills its victim so quickly that, once in the grip of the scorpion, the prey has almost no chance of freeing itself. And any human unlucky enough to be stung is in for an extremely painful experience: Deathstalker venom attacks the nervous system, lungs, and heart, causing convulsions, paralysis, and even death. If you spot one, stay far away!

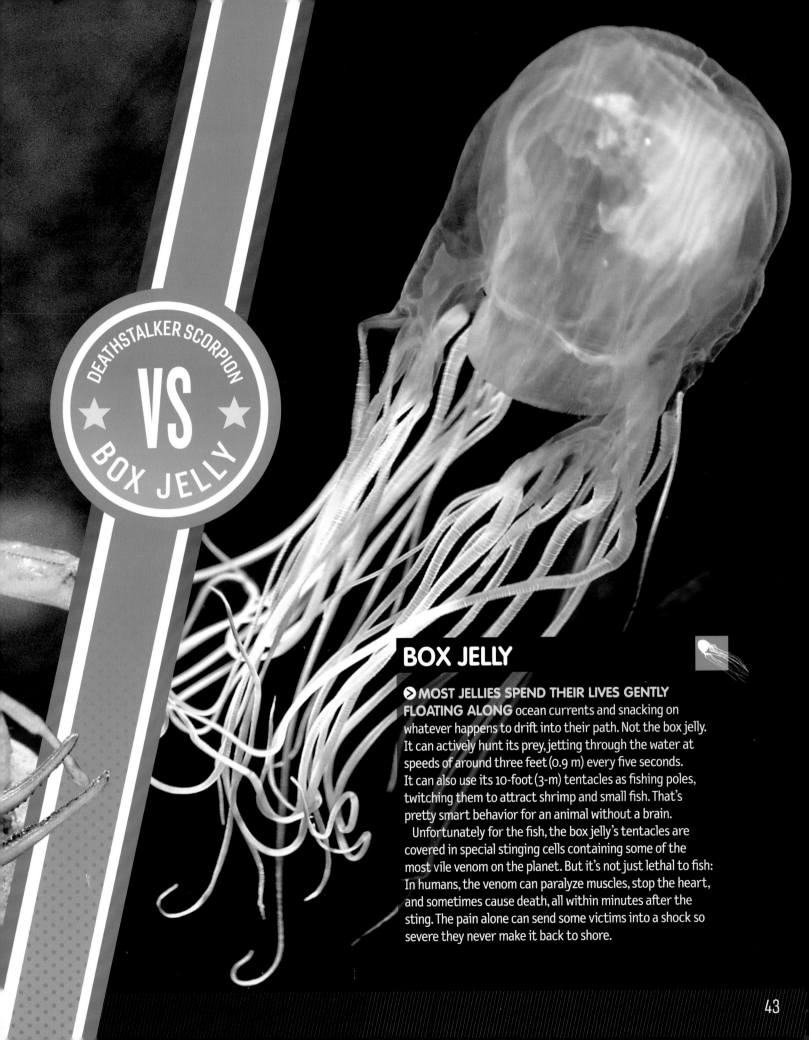

DEATHSTALKER SCORPION ★ VS ★ BOX JELLY

BOX JELLY

❯ MOST JELLIES SPEND THEIR LIVES GENTLY FLOATING ALONG ocean currents and snacking on whatever happens to drift into their path. Not the box jelly. It can actively hunt its prey, jetting through the water at speeds of around three feet (0.9 m) every five seconds. It can also use its 10-foot (3-m) tentacles as fishing poles, twitching them to attract shrimp and small fish. That's pretty smart behavior for an animal without a brain.

Unfortunately for the fish, the box jelly's tentacles are covered in special stinging cells containing some of the most vile venom on the planet. But it's not just lethal to fish: In humans, the venom can paralyze muscles, stop the heart, and sometimes cause death, all within minutes after the sting. The pain alone can send some victims into a shock so severe they never make it back to shore.

You might want to **KEEP ON THESE CREATURES' GOOD SIDE.**

SCIENTISTS MADE A **CHEMICAL** BASED ON DEATHSTALKER VENOM THAT MAKES CANCER CELLS **GLOW.** THIS HELPS SURGEONS REMOVE TUMORS MORE EASILY.

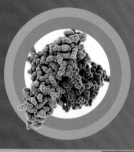

INSIDE THE VENOM
Scorpion venom gets its paralyzing power from a special molecule that blocks certain chemicals from entering muscle cells. Normally, those chemicals tell muscles to relax. But because the chemicals can't reach their target, all the muscles in the body flex out of control.

PUNY PINCERS, BIG STING
One way to judge the power of a scorpion's venom is by looking at its pincers. Scorpions with big pincers can subdue their prey simply by grabbing it, so they don't need strong venom. Scorpions with small pincers, like the deathstalker, need powerful venom to make up for their weak grip.

In 2017, researchers filmed **SCORPIONS STRIKING** with high-speed video and then rewatched the tapes in slow motion. They found that the deathstalkers' strike was the fastest of all seven species they tested, **MOVING AT 51 INCHES (130 CM) PER SECOND!**

DEATHSTALKER SCORPION

COMMON NAME:	DEATHSTALKER SCORPION	SCIENTIFIC NAME:	LEIURUS QUINQUESTRIATUS

SIZE:
UP TO
3.9 INCHES
(10 CM) LONG

WHERE THEY LIVE:
THE DESERTS AND
SCRUBLANDS
OF NORTHERN AFRICA AND THE MIDDLE EAST

SELF-DEFENSE

The box jelly's terrible toxin plays a very important role in the jelly's safety. Jellies have incredibly delicate bodies that could easily be torn apart by a thrashing fish. The jelly's swift-acting venom prevents the prey from struggling and damaging its tentacles.

MOST JELLIES CAN'T SEE, so they can only sting what they're lucky enough to bump into. But BOX JELLIES HAVE DEVELOPED EYES—24 OF THEM! As for how they know what they're looking at without a brain, scientists are baffled.

STING STATS

A box jelly can have up to 15 tentacles growing from each corner of its bell, or its cube-shaped body. Each tentacle has about 5,000 barbed venom-containing cells.

BOX JELLY

WINNER

| COMMON NAME: | BOX JELLY | SCIENTIFIC NAME: | CLASS CUBOZOA |

SIZE:

10 FEET (3 M) LONG,
12 INCHES
(30 CM) ACROSS

WHERE THEY LIVE:

COASTAL WATERS OF NORTHERN
AUSTRALIA
AND THROUGHOUT THE INDO-PACIFIC

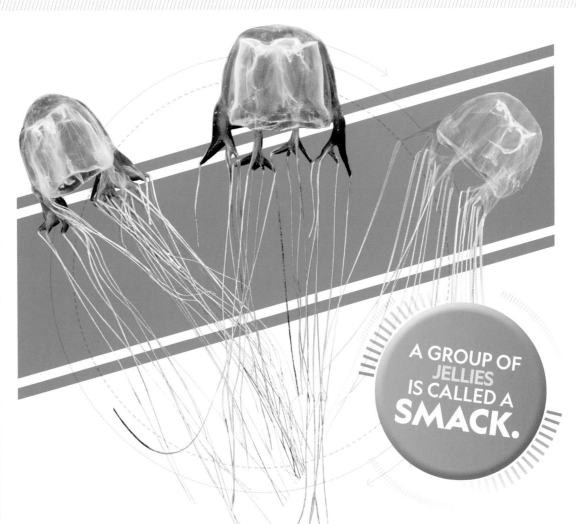

A GROUP OF JELLIES IS CALLED A **SMACK.**

Getting stung by either of these viciously venomous creatures is no picnic. Both can cause humans excruciating pain and sometimes death. But when it comes to which is worse, the prize goes to the box jelly. Unlike a deathstalker scorpion's venom, which affects human muscles, box jelly venom attacks the heart, nervous system, and even the skin cells. **THAT MAKES THE BOX JELLY THE MOST VENOMOUS ANIMAL IN THE SEA—AND POSSIBLY THE MOST TOXIC CREATURE ON EARTH.**

EXTREME-LY TOXIC CRITTERS

YOU'LL WANT TO KEEP YOUR DISTANCE FROM THESE POISONOUS, VENOMOUS, AND PAIN-PRODUCING ANIMALS.

BRAZILIAN WANDERING SPIDER

Not content to sit in a web and wait for prey to come their way, Brazilian wandering spiders roam the forest floor at night, hunting. Though their bite is intensely painful and can be deadly to humans, **THESE SPIDERS PREFER TO STRIKE INSECTS, OTHER SPIDERS, REPTILES, AND MICE.**

HOODED PITOHUI

Sure, there are poisonous fish and frogs. But a poisonous *bird*? The hooded pitohui is one of the world's only toxic birds. Its **FEATHERS HOLD AN EXTREMELY POWERFUL TOXIN—** the same substance that allows poison dart frogs to pack their famous, fatal punch.

KOMODO DRAGON

At up to **366 POUNDS (166 KG) AND MORE THAN 10 FEET (3 M) LONG,** these are the largest lizards in the world—and they're also venomous. **POWERFUL VENOM IN THE KOMODO'S SALIVA** means that a bite will cause even large prey, such as deer, to weaken and die within a few days. Then, the dragon uses its powerful sense of smell to track down its meal.

PLATYPUS

The platypus is such a weird animal that the first scientists to examine one thought someone was trying to trick them. In addition to their duck-like bills and beaver-like tails, **MALE PLATYPUSES HAVE VENOMOUS STINGERS ON THE HEELS OF THEIR HIND FEET.** The platypus's venom produces a searing pain that scientists can't yet erase with painkillers.

KING COBRA

It's not just one of the most venomous snakes in the world—it's also the longest of all venomous snakes, stretching up to 18 feet (5.5 m). It's so big it can raise up the front of its body and look an adult human in the eye. **A SINGLE BITE FROM THE SUPERSIZE SNAKE CAN KILL AN ELEPHANT.** *Yikes!*

STONEFISH

There are about 1,200 species of venomous fish—so it's really saying something that the stonefish is one of the deadliest of all. Worse, they blend in so perfectly with the rocky reefs where they live that even scuba divers have trouble spotting them. **EACH OF THE 13 SPINES ON A STONEFISH'S BACK CAN DELIVER ENOUGH TOXIN TO KILL A HUMAN WITHIN AN HOUR.**

MOST PROTECTIVE

THESE ANIMALS TAKE CAREGIVING TO THE NEXT LEVEL.

But which should be crowned **BEST CAREGIVER?**

ORANGUTAN

▶ **HIGH UP IN A TREE IN THE RAINFORESTS OF SUMATRA,** a mother orangutan cradles her newborn baby in her arms. The infant has a pinkish face and a tuft of hair that stands straight up. Though orangutans are a mostly solitary species, mother and offspring have an extremely tight bond.

Orangutan babies stay in close contact with their mothers for many years. Offspring often live with their moms in the same tree until about the age of seven or eight—longer than any of the other great apes. Even after becoming independent, female offspring will often visit their mothers until they're 15 or 16 years old, when they start having babies of their own. Those are some strong family ties!

STRAWBERRY POISON DART FROG

> **A FROG MAY NOT BE THE FIRST ANIMAL YOU THINK OF WHEN IT COMES TO ANIMAL FAMILIES.** But the strawberry poison dart frog is devoted to keeping its tadpoles safe so they can grow into adults.

This amphibian is a poison dart frog, one of the most toxic animals alive. The frog extracts deadly compounds from the mites, ants, beetles, and millipedes it dines on. Then, it stores those compounds in glands in its skin. If a predator looms too close, the frog can secrete the toxins. Anything daring enough to take a bite is in big trouble. That makes this animal the perfect bodyguard for its young.

ORANGUTAN
VS
STRAWBERRY
POISON DART FROG

Which critter is the most PROTECTIVE?

MALE AND FEMALE BABY ORANGUTANS LOOK SIMILAR, BUT THE MALES GROW UP TO BE **THREE TIMES** THE WEIGHT OF ADULT FEMALES!

ORANGUTAN

| COMMON NAME: | **ORANGUTAN** | SCIENTIFIC NAME: | **GENUS PONGO** |

SIZE:

UP TO

5 FEET (1.5 M) TALL

WHERE THEY LIVE:

ON THE SOUTHEAST ASIAN ISLANDS OF

SUMATRA

AND BORNEO

PIGGYBACK RIDES

For the first few weeks after they're born, baby orangutans constantly cling to their mother's belly as she moves through the treetops. Then, they switch to riding on her back so they can observe what's going on around them. Youngsters ride piggyback until about age four or five, when they're able to move around the rainforest on their own.

Orangutans communicate with each other using a **COMPLEX SYSTEM OF VOCALIZATIONS.** Researchers have found that there are at least 32 of them, from a "kiss-squeak" to a "grumph." **MOTHERS MAKE A SOFT, SCRAPING NOISE** to tell their youngsters to keep close.

LIFE LESSONS

Momma orangutans have a lot to teach their youngsters. Watching their mother forage helps little orangutans develop a mental map of where all the fruit trees in their range are located and remember when they bear fruit. They also learn from their mom how to build nests for sleeping—a skill so tricky it takes about three years to master!

STRAWBERRY POISON DART FROG

COMMON NAME: STRAWBERRY POISON DART FROG **SCIENTIFIC NAME:** OOPHAGA PUMILIO

SIZE:

0.7 to 0.9 INCHES (18–23 MM)

WHERE THEY LIVE:

RAINFORESTS OF CENTRAL
AMERICA

DEVOTED DADS
A female strawberry poison dart frog lays her eggs on the forest floor—but the eggs must be kept moist or they'll die. That's where Dad comes in. He hauls water to the eggs in a special pouch. He also removes fungus from the eggs and carefully rotates them each day so they get enough oxygen.

HARDWORKING MOMS
When the eggs hatch, Mom takes over caregiving duties from Dad. One at a time, she hitches each tadpole onto her back and carries it to its own small pool in the water-filled hollow of a plant called a bromeliad. There, the tiny tadpole slowly develops into a frog.

Every day, the mother brings her babies a **TO-GO LUNCH. SHE FEEDS THEM HER UNFERTILIZED EGGS,** which provide the tadpoles with not only nutrients but also the poison they'll use for protection. The frog is the first animal known to pass on this kind of **CHEMICAL DEFENSE TO ITS OFFSPRING.**

MALE STRAWBERRY POISON DART FROGS **WRESTLE** EACH OTHER TO PROTECT THEIR TERRITORY.

This showdown is almost too close to call. Though orangutans are well known for spending years caring for their offspring, the strawberry poison dart frog also scores high marks in the devoted caregiver department. And the mother and father amphibian go to great lengths for their offspring even before they hatch, tending to them all the way from egg to tadpole to adult frog. **WINNER: STRAWBERRY POISON DART FROG.**

LONGEST LIVING

HUMANS ARE NO SLACKERS WHEN IT COMES TO AGING.

But compared to these LONG-LIVING ANIMALS, even the oldest humans seem like spring chickens.

BOWHEAD WHALE

❯ THE BOWHEAD WHALE IS AN EXTREME CREATURE. For starters, it's enormous, weighing up to 100 tons (91 t), and it sports a 1.6-foot (0.5-m)-thick layer of insulating blubber. The whale also boasts a huge head—which is more than a third of its body length—that it uses to break through Arctic ice up to eight inches (20 cm) thick.

Yet the most incredible thing about this creature might be its age. Scientists once thought that bowheads had a similar life span to other whales. But then they began noticing something strange: Many of these whales were swimming around with stubs of odd materials embedded in their skin, like slate, metal, and ivory. Analysis revealed that they were the tips of old harpoon points left behind when hunters tried—and failed—to take down the whales more than a hundred years ago. But just how old can these mega-mammals get?

AMERICAN LOBSTER

> **IN 2007, PHOTOS OF LOBSTERS WITH CAPTIONS CLAIMING THE ANIMALS WERE "BIOLOGICALLY IMMORTAL" WENT VIRAL.** Then in 2008, fishermen made a surprising find. They captured a supersize, 20-pound (9-kg) American lobster off the coast of Newfoundland, Canada, and sold it to a New York City seafood restaurant. It turned out that the creature was much more than a delicious dish—it was a scientific marvel estimated to be 140 years old! (The estimate was made based on the lobster's whopping weight.) The restaurant owner named the lobster George and refused to make a meal out of him. George was released back into the sea to grow even older.

So, were the internet stories right? Could lobsters like George really live forever? No way, say scientists! However, they do age differently than most other creatures on Earth. And they can have unusually long lives—just ask George!

BOWHEAD WHALE
★ VS ★
AMERICAN LOBSTER

These animals better be getting SENIOR DISCOUNTS.

A BOWHEAD WHALE'S TAIL CAN STRETCH **25 FEET (7.6 M)** ACROSS, FROM ONE FLUKE TIP TO THE OTHER.

WINNER

BOWHEAD WHALE

| COMMON NAME: | BOWHEAD WHALE | SCIENTIFIC NAME: | BALAENA MYSTICETUS |

SIZE:

66 FEET
(20 M)

WHERE THEY LIVE:

THE
ARCTIC

Bowhead whales have unusual **MUTATIONS IN THEIR GENES** that scientists think may help with repairing DNA damage. That might protect them from all kinds of diseases, including cancer, making it easier for the **WHALES TO LIVE TO A RIPE OLD AGE.**

OLD-TIMER

By testing the eyeballs of 48 bowhead whales for a substance called aspartic acid (which increases with age), scientists found that most of the whales lived between 20 and 60 years. But a few lived much longer— including one that lived to be an astounding 211 years old.

CHILL OUT

Why do the whales live so long? Scientists think it may have something to do with their lifestyle. Bowheads inhabit the frigid Arctic. There, the cold environment causes their metabolisms (the chemical processes that occur in their bodies) to work very slowly, extending their life span.

AMERICAN LOBSTER

COMMON NAME:	**AMERICAN LOBSTER**	SCIENTIFIC NAME:	**HOMARUS AMERICANUS**

SIZE:

UP TO

3.25 FEET

(1 M) LONG

WHERE THEY LIVE:

ALONG MUCH OF NORTH AMERICA'S

ATLANTIC COAST

IMMORTAL ANIMAL?

While no lobsters, including American lobsters, are immortal, they don't show the signs of aging that most creatures do. Lobsters never stop reproducing, lose strength, or slow their eating, even in old age.

Lobsters also NEVER STOP GROWING. That might seem odd to us humans, who don't get any taller after we reach adulthood. But there are many organisms, including some crustaceans, barnacles, and water fleas called daphnia, that simply KEEP GETTING BIGGER.

HOW MANY BIRTHDAY CANDLES?

As a lobster grows, it regularly sheds its exoskeleton to form a new, larger one. That means experts can't use an exoskeleton to tell a lobster's age. They used to estimate age based on a lobster's size. But in 2012, researchers found that American lobsters develop internal "growth rings"—sort of like trees! This will help provide more data on just how old these guys can get.

DEPENDING ON THEIR SIZE, FEMALE AMERICAN LOBSTERS CAN PRODUCE **5,000 TO MORE THAN 100,000 EGGS** AT A TIME.

Happy birthday to ... who? Both these creatures boast a life span that can top a century. That means some American lobsters and bowhead whales alive today have been around since about the year 1920. But when it comes to which old-timer is most impressive, **THE WINNER IS THE WHALE.** Bowheads age so well that scientists are currently studying their DNA in the hopes of finding the secrets to living a longer, healthier life.

EXTREME-LY GREAT GRAND-ANIMALS

STEP ASIDE, GRANDPA.

These ancient animals are some of the **LONGEST-LIVING** species on the planet.

ALDABRA GIANT TORTOISE

The current record holder for the world's oldest known land animal is a giant tortoise called Jonathan. At **MORE THAN 180 YEARS OLD,** Jonathan enjoys a luxurious retirement, living on the grounds of the governor's mansion on the island of St. Helena in the South Atlantic Ocean.

KAKAPO PARROT

The kakapo's short wings are just for show: This is the **WORLD'S ONLY FLIGHTLESS PARROT!** They are also perhaps the world's longest-living bird, reaching **AROUND 90 YEARS OF AGE** on average. Unfortunately, they are also critically endangered, despite living in semicaptivity on two predator-free islands off New Zealand. Fewer than 200 of the birds are left.

GREENLAND SHARK

Reaching 24 feet (7.3 m) long and weighing in at up to **2,200 POUNDS (1,000 KG)**, the Greenland shark is one of the largest sharks on Earth. These fish are sluggish swimmers, but they can keep going—and going and going! Scientists are just beginning to study the shark's longevity, but it's estimated they **MIGHT BE ABLE TO LIVE LONGER THAN 272 YEARS.**

LAYSAN ALBATROSS

THE OLDEST KNOWN WILD BIRD is a Laysan albatross nicknamed "Wisdom" that scientists estimate to be at least 68 years old. Not only that, but she's still laying eggs. (Laysan females lay just one egg at a time.) Researchers, who have been tracking the bird since 1956, believe she has **LAID MORE THAN 30 EGGS IN HER LIFETIME.**

QUAHOG CLAM

Like the American lobster, quahog clams have **"GROWTH RINGS" FOR EVERY YEAR THEY'VE BEEN ALIVE.** Quahogs often live to around 100, but when scientists counted the rings of one quahog dredged up from chilly Arctic waters in 2006, they were shocked. The clam, nicknamed Ming, was 507 years old. That means it hatched in the year 1499!

MOST COOPERATIVE

YOU AND YOUR FRIENDS MIGHT BE CLOSE.

But unless you walk around in FORMATION or let your buddies USE YOUR BODY AS A BRIDGE, you're falling short of these creature crews.

CANADA GOOSE

> **A DARK SHAPE APPEARS IN THE SKY, QUICKLY MOVING CLOSER.** You squint to get a better look. Is it an airplane? Then you hear it: *Honk! Honk! Honk!* It's the unmistakable sound of a flock of geese. They're migrating, flying from the north to the southern United States and Mexico for the winter.

As the geese go, they keep a tight, V-shaped formation. A closer look reveals that the lead goose flies the lowest, with each goose behind it slightly higher than the one in front. Moving in this way helps them cover as many as 1,500 miles (2,414 km) in just 24 hours! But why do Canada geese turn air travel into a team event?

HONEYBEE

▶ *BUZZZZZ*. A HONEYBEE BOBS HER WAY THROUGH A GARDEN. She goes from flower to flower, busily dipping her tongue into the nectar and slurping it up. As she travels, the flowers' pollen sticks to her hairy legs and body. Later, she will groom herself, depositing the pollen into pouches on her hind legs. After she's collected enough pollen and nectar, she makes her way back to the hive.

There wait the rest of the bees in her colony: a single queen and several hundred males called drones. A drone's main job is to help keep the population of the hive stable by reproducing with the queen. Most people never see these bees because they don't leave the hive. The workers (all females) must not only feed themselves but also gather enough supplies for the whole hive. And that's just one of the ways these incredible insects work together.

CANADA GOOSE
★ VS ★
HONEYBEE

These creatures are CHAMPIONS OF COOPERATION.

CANADA GOOSE GOSLINGS CAN TRAVEL IN GROUPS OF **UP TO 100.**

CANADA GOOSE

COMMON NAME:	CANADA GOOSE	SCIENTIFIC NAME:	BRANTA CANADENSIS

SIZE:

BODY: 30 TO **43** INCHES (76–109 CM)

WINGSPAN: 4.2 TO **5.6** FEET (1.3–1.7 M)

WHERE THEY LIVE:

ACROSS NORTH **AMERICA**

Geese travel in their **V-SHAPED PATTERN** for an important reason: It **HELPS THEM CONSERVE ENERGY.** By flying behind and slightly above the goose in front of it, each bird faces reduced wind resistance. Flying like this means the group can **COVER 71 PERCENT MORE DISTANCE** than a solo goose!

TAKE YOUR TURN
The goose at the front of the V has to face the wind head-on. This position requires extra energy, but these fliers play fair: They trade off being in front, falling back when they get tired.

SQUAD GOALS
The V formation also helps the geese keep track of each other. Flying in a tight pattern makes it easy to keep tabs on every goose in the group so nobody gets lost. Fighter pilots use the V formation for the same reason.

HONEYBEE

WINNER

COMMON NAME:	HONEYBEE	SCIENTIFIC NAME:	APIS MELLIFERA

SIZE:

WORKERS ARE

0.4 to 0.6 INCHES
(10–15 MM)

WHERE THEY LIVE:

ACROSS MOST OF THE

WORLD

I'LL "BEE" YOUR BRIDGE
If there's a space in the hive too big to cross, honeybees will work together to bridge the gap with their bodies. They link hooks on their legs to the hooks of the next bee, forming a chain with their bodies so other bees can walk across.

Honeybees work together to REGULATE THE TEMPERATURE INSIDE THE HIVE. When it's too hot, they'll all fan their wings. When it's too cold, they'll gather into a basketball-shaped cluster and take turns warming up in the toasty center.

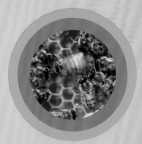

DANCE PARTY OF ONE
When one bee finds a food source, she will come back to the hive and perform an intricate "waggle dance" to communicate the directions to the food and how far it is from the hive. Since the hive is pitch-black, other bees hold their antennae close to the dancing bee to sense the vibrations of her movement.

BEES BEAT THEIR WINGS ABOUT **200 TIMES A SECOND.**

A flock of Canada geese flying in formation like a fleet of turbo-powered airplanes is an impressive sight. But when it comes to which animal has superior teamwork, **THE TITLE GOES TO THE HONEYBEE.** Each bee in the hive depends on the rest for survival. They work together in every aspect of life, from finding food to building their hive to raising their young. In fact, honeybees rely on each other so deeply that scientists say a colony of honeybees is more like one single "superorganism" than a group of individuals. Go team!

HARDIEST SURVIVOR

WHICH OF EARTH'S CREATURES CAN KEEP ON GOING, EVEN UNDER CONDITIONS THAT WOULD MAKE OTHERS CALL IT QUITS?

THESE BEASTS can beat out **EXTREME CONDITIONS** to survive and even thrive.

COCKROACH

YOU FLIP ON THE LIGHT IN THE MIDDLE OF THE NIGHT AND SPOT A DARK SHAPE SCURRYING ACROSS THE FLOOR. *EEEP!* A cockroach! Nobody wants a germ-laden cockroach in their kitchen. But in reality, the roaches were here first. They are ancient insects that have been on Earth for about 300 million years. In that time, they've had to outlast all kinds of catastrophic events—including the mass extinction that wiped out almost all the dinosaurs about 66 million years ago. Cockroaches are incredibly hardy creatures, able to survive on almost anything, including glue, soap, and leather. They can go a month without food and more than a week without water. That's one impressive insect!

CAMEL

❯ IN THE DESERT, THE SUN RISES LIKE A BRIGHT ORANGE FIREBALL. Soon, it's scorching the ground and heating the air to a withering 120°F (49°C). There's nothing but sand stretching in every direction. Food and water are nearly nonexistent. Yet there's one animal that seems totally comfortable in these extreme conditions: the camel.

There are two species of camel: the dromedary, which has one hump and lives in North Africa and the Middle East, and the Bactrian, which has two humps and lives in Central Asia. Both are incredibly tough. They can carry more than 200 pounds (91 kg) and go more than a week without water and more than a month without food. To survive on so little, they can drop 40 percent of their body weight without serious problems. How do they do it?

COCKROACH
★ VS ★
CAMEL

Which critter can TOUGH IT OUT like no other?

COCKROACHES CAN RUN UP TO **3.4 MILES AN HOUR** (5.5 KM/H).

WINNER

COCKROACH

COMMON NAME:	COCKROACH	SCIENTIFIC NAME:	ORDER BLATTODEA

SIZE:

UP TO

2 INCHES
(5 CM) LONG

WHERE THEY LIVE:

ANYWHERE

HUMANS
LIVE

Roaches can go for long periods not only **WITHOUT FOOD AND WATER** but also **WITHOUT AIR.** They can hold their breath for five to seven minutes at a time, and they can **SURVIVE FOR SEVERAL MINUTES UNDERWATER.**

NO HEAD, NO PROBLEM
It sounds like a horrifying myth, but it's true: Roaches can survive for weeks after losing their heads. That's because they don't breathe through their mouths: Instead, they take in and expel air using a system of little holes in each body segment.

DEATH-DEFYING
Roaches can even outsmart us to survive. In the mid-1980s, exterminators started mixing sugary bait with roach poison to try to wipe out the vermin. But in 1993, it stopped working. The roaches had evolved at super speed, tweaking their taste buds so that sugar tasted bitter to them—and so that they stayed away from traps.

STORAGE SYSTEM

Let's set the record straight: A camel's hump does not hold water. In fact, it stores fat, which can be used for nutrition when food is scarce—a common problem in the desert. When a camel has used up its fat reserves, its hump deflates and flops over to one side.

BIG GULP

When camels find water, they have to stock up. Camels can drink around 30 gallons (114 L)—enough to fill a small bathtub—in one go! A human would not be able to survive drinking that amount of water at once. But camels have unusual red blood cells that can puff up to store water without bursting.

MOST CREATURES LOSE WATER THROUGH THEIR WASTE AND THROUGH BREATHING. But in the dry desert, animals need to hold on to as much moisture as possible. **CAMELS' URINE IS SO CONCENTRATED IT'S THE CONSISTENCY OF SYRUP;** their poo is dry; and they have special structures inside their noses that absorb water from their exhaled air.

CAMEL

COMMON NAME:	CAMEL	SCIENTIFIC NAME:	GENUS CAMELUS

SIZE:

1,600 TO **1,800** POUNDS (726–816 KG)

WHERE THEY LIVE:

NORTH AFRICA, THE MIDDLE EAST, AND **CENTRAL** ASIA

IN 2001, SCIENTISTS DISCOVERED A NEW SPECIES OF CAMEL THAT SURVIVES BY **DRINKING SALT WATER.**

A camel's survival skills are pretty impressive. These creatures are so robust that in the 1850s, the U.S. military experimented with using them as pack animals in the American Southwest. The camels could carry a 700-pound (318-kg) load for days on end without stopping for food or water. But the roach is even more rugged: It can eat almost anything, keep living without a head, and—as one experiment showed—even survive the extreme radiation of a nuclear explosion. **THAT MAKES ROACHES THE WINNER.**

EXTREME-LY DURABLE SURVIVORS

THESE ANIMALS CAN *SURVIVE* ALMOST ANYTHING.

TARDIGRADE

What critter is as tiny as it is tough? Meet the tardigrade, a **MICROSCOPIC CREATURE THAT CAN SURVIVE BEING BOILED, DRIED OUT, FROZEN, AND HIT WITH INTENSE RADIATION.** Scientists have even tried blasting a bunch of tardigrades into space. Some of the creatures didn't survive. But many of the itty-bitty astronauts returned to Earth, appearing to be totally unfazed by their space mission.

CLIMBING PERCH

Talk about a **FISH OUT OF WATER!** If the climbing perch's pond goes dry, it can survive in the dry bottom for six months as it waits for rain to come. Or it can take matters into its own fins, **CRAWLING ACROSS LAND FOR UP TO SIX DAYS AT A TIME** to look for a new water source.

MOUNTAIN STONE WETA

This is one big insect—about **FOUR INCHES (10 CM) LONG,** even without its antennae and legs. But that's not what makes it so tough. The New Zealand native can **SURVIVE BEING FROZEN IN ICE FOR HOURS AT A TIME.**

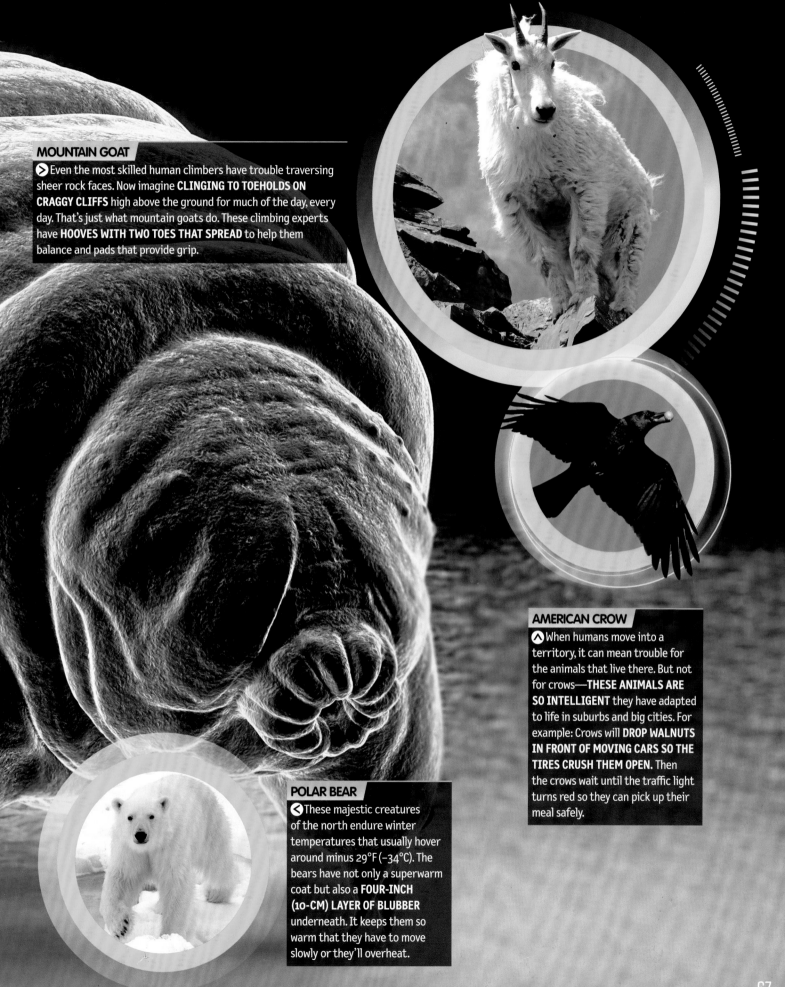

MOUNTAIN GOAT

▸ Even the most skilled human climbers have trouble traversing sheer rock faces. Now imagine **CLINGING TO TOEHOLDS ON CRAGGY CLIFFS** high above the ground for much of the day, every day. That's just what mountain goats do. These climbing experts have **HOOVES WITH TWO TOES THAT SPREAD** to help them balance and pads that provide grip.

AMERICAN CROW

▲ When humans move into a territory, it can mean trouble for the animals that live there. But not for crows—**THESE ANIMALS ARE SO INTELLIGENT** they have adapted to life in suburbs and big cities. For example: Crows will **DROP WALNUTS IN FRONT OF MOVING CARS SO THE TIRES CRUSH THEM OPEN.** Then the crows wait until the traffic light turns red so they can pick up their meal safely.

POLAR BEAR

◂ These majestic creatures of the north endure winter temperatures that usually hover around minus 29°F (–34°C). The bears have not only a superwarm coat but also a **FOUR-INCH (10-CM) LAYER OF BLUBBER** underneath. It keeps them so warm that they have to move slowly or they'll overheat.

BEST DIGGER

MANY ANIMALS DIG HOLES,

but most BURROWS are no more than simple hollows in the earth. That's not the case for these EXPERT EXCAVATORS.

GROUNDHOG

> **ONCE A YEAR, GROUNDHOGS BECOME CELEBRITIES.** On February 2, people across the United States wait breathlessly for the most watched weather forecast of the year—one that's made by a rodent! According to legend, if a groundhog emerges from its underground hiding place to see its shadow, there will be six more weeks of winter. If not, spring is near.

In reality, groundhogs aren't the most reliable meteorologists, but they do have other talents. Groundhogs hibernate the winter away in burrows that they dig in the ground. These subsurface shelters are much more than just a place to nap: They provide protection from predators such as dogs, coyotes, and foxes. And groundhogs are skilled burrowers, using their long, sharp claws to create underground lairs that are nothing short of elaborate.

GROUNDHOG VS NILE CROCODILE

NILE CROCODILE

> **THEY CAN BE 20 FEET (6 M) LONG AND WEIGH UP TO 1,650 POUNDS (748 KG)—AS MUCH AS A HORSE!** These fearsome predators mostly eat fish but will chow down on almost anything that crosses their path, including zebras, small hippos, and even other crocodiles.

But for all their ferocity, Nile crocodiles have one vulnerability: Like all reptiles, they are exothermic, or cold-blooded. Unlike mammals, they don't produce their own heat, but instead must rely on the heat of the sun to warm their bodies. The crocs can often be spotted basking in the sunlight along riverbanks. But what's a giant, cold-blooded animal to do when chilly weather strikes? The answer: Dig deep.

Time to DIG IN with these incredible excavators.

ONCE A GROUNDHOG HAS **MOVED OUT** OF ITS BURROW, OTHER ANIMALS—SUCH AS RABBITS, CHIPMUNKS, AND SNAKES—OFTEN **MOVE IN.**

GROUNDHOG

COMMON NAME:	**GROUNDHOG**	SCIENTIFIC NAME:	**MARMOTA MONAX**

SIZE:

16 to 27 INCHES
(41–69 CM) LONG

WHERE THEY LIVE:

PARTS OF THE UNITED STATES AND
CANADA

Groundhog burrows often have **MULTIPLE EXITS AND MANY CHAMBERS INSIDE,** providing a home for several groundhog roommates. One part of the burrow is for hibernating, and another part is for napping. **THEY EVEN HAVE SEPARATE BATHROOMS!**

UNDERGROUND FORTRESS
With a top speed of eight miles an hour (12.9 km/h), groundhogs aren't nearly fast enough to outrun speedy predators like hawks and coyotes. A burrow provides the perfect hideout for these slowpokes. Besides providing protection, burrows are where the rodents sleep and raise their young.

NICE DIGS
For such a small animal, a groundhog's burrow is pretty impressive: It can have up to 66 feet (20 m) of tunnels buried up to six feet (1.8 m) underground. Some groundhogs even have multiple residences—how fancy!

NILE CROCODILE

SAFE AND SOUND

One reason crocs dig holes is to create a protected place to lay their eggs. Females dig nesting holes about 20 inches (51 cm) deep in the banks of a body of water and then lay between 20 and 80 eggs.

Nile crocodiles also dig for another reason. When temperatures get too cold, they'll **USE THEIR SNOUTS AND FEET TO BURROW DOWN INTO THE EARTH.** Then, they enter a sleeplike state called **ESTIVATION THAT'S SIMILAR TO HIBERNATION.**

HOW DEEP?

Small crocodiles will dig burrows as deep as 12 feet (3.7 m) and then spend months just chilling out, their hearts beating only twice a minute. Bigger, older crocs go even deeper—up to 39 feet (12 m)! Then they usually only come up to the surface during the warmest part of the day to bask in the sun.

COMMON NAME:	NILE CROCODILE	SCIENTIFIC NAME:	CROCODYLUS NILOTICUS

SIZE:

AVERAGE OF

16 FEET
(4.9 M)

WHERE THEY LIVE:

RIVERS, MARSHES, AND SWAMPS IN SUB-SAHARAN AFRICA,

THE NILE BASIN,
AND MADAGASCAR

UNLIKE MOST OTHER REPTILES, NILE CROCODILES **GUARD THEIR EGGS** UNTIL THEY HATCH.

Which critter will dig its way to victory? Sure, groundhogs are well known for their burrowing skills, and their underground hideouts are even part of an annual holiday tradition. But when it comes to deepness, their homes are downright shallow at five feet (1.5 m). Though the Nile crocodile doesn't seem like it could beat anyone in a shoveling contest, the reptile blows away the competition by digging down to five times the depth of the average swimming pool! **THAT'S WHY THE CROCODILE SNAPS UP THIS WIN.**

EXTREME-LY *IMPRESSIVE BURROWERS*

We may spend our days on Earth's surface, but there's a whole other world **BENEATH OUR FEET.**

MEET SOME ANIMALS THAT LIVE MYSTERIOUS LIVES UNDERGROUND.

BURROWING OWL

Most owls nest high up in trees, but these little birds do things a little differently. Burrowing owls let other animals, such as tortoises and armadillos, do the digging, taking over the holes when those critters abandon them. **THE OWLS THEN "DECORATE" THEIR NEW HOMES WITH GRASS AND FEATHERS.**

JERBOA

These **BIG-EARED, MOUSE-LIKE CREATURES** live in the deserts and steppes of eastern Europe, Asia, and northern Africa. To beat the heat, they spend the daylight hours in burrows. Some species **PLUG THEIR BURROW ENTRANCES WITH SOIL WHEN THEY LEAVE TO KEEP THE INSIDES COOL** while they're gone.

GILA MONSTER

No, the Gila monster isn't *actually* a monster. At up to two feet (0.6 m) long, it's the **LARGEST LIZARD** native to the United States and one of only a handful of venomous lizards in the world. These homebodies **SPEND 95 PERCENT OF THEIR LIVES IN BURROWS** they dig in their desert homes, emerging briefly in the springtime to eat.

AARDVARK

These African critters have **SHOVEL-LIKE CLAWS** that can dig at a rate of two feet (0.6 m) in just 15 seconds. They use them to make burrows and also to break through termite mounds to feast on the tasty insects inside.

EARTHWORM

Earthworms seem like pretty low-key critters, quietly **WRIGGLING THROUGH THE SOIL.** But they perform a very important service: They break down decaying leaves and grass into nutrients that plants can use and add them to the ground. Earthworms are so important for healthy soil that they're called **"ECOSYSTEM ENGINEERS!"**

MEERKAT

These social critters **LIVE IN GROUPS OF UP TO 40 INDIVIDUALS,** all sharing one intricate burrow. Their homes have an average of 15 entrances and exits, several levels of tunnels, and **BATHROOM AND SLEEPING CHAMBERS.**

BEST HAIRDO

Humans can rock **BRAIDS, POMPADOURS, MOHAWKS,** and much more. (After all, we're one of the few animals that sport a crop of hair on our heads!)

BUT OUR HAIRSTYLES ARE NOTHING SPECIAL COMPARED TO THE HAIRDOS OF THESE FASHIONABLE CREATURES.

HAIRY FROGFISH

❯ IT MIGHT JUST BE THE MOST FABULOUS FISH IN THE SEA. The hairy frogfish's furry appearance helps it hide on the ocean floor, blending in perfectly with coral reefs in the warm, tropical waters where it lives. The frogfish's sneaky camouflage makes it highly skilled at ambushing prey. When it sees a potential snack, such as a crustacean or small fish, it lunges from its hiding place. Then, GULP! Hairy frogfish can swallow prey their own length. What's more, spotting and snapping up this fast-food meal can take a mere six milliseconds—compare that to the average human reaction time of more than 200 milliseconds! Oddly, it's the frogfish's remarkable hairstyle that makes its extreme eating habits possible.

MACARONI PENGUIN

WHEN YOU THINK OF A PENGUIN, a bird wearing plain black and white might come to mind. But the macaroni penguin sports an outfit other penguins might call outlandish. The orange-yellow crest on its head begins between its eyes and extends backward in a V shape. No hair gel required!

The macaroni penguin's bright yellow hairdo really stands out in the snowy Antarctic, where these penguins make their home. Macaroni penguins spend six months of the year at sea, but during breeding season, they head for the shore to build nests made of small stones or pebbles. They gather in dense colonies that can number 100,000 individuals. That's a lot of good hair!

HAIRY FROGFISH
VS
MACARONI PENGUIN

For these cool critters, EVERY DAY IS A GOOD HAIR DAY.

FROGFISH CAN GET AROUND BY USING THEIR FINS TO **"WALK"** ALONG THE SEAFLOOR.

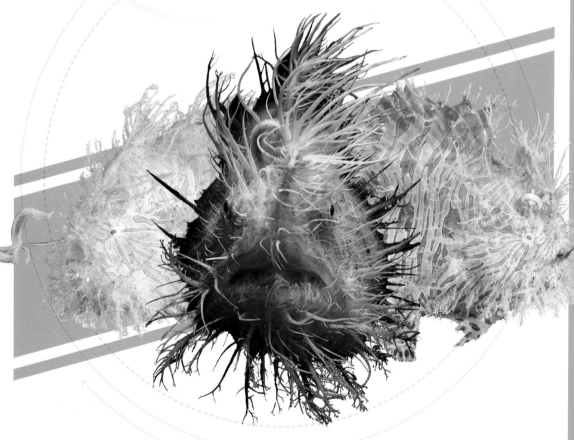

HAIRY FROGFISH

WINNER

COMMON NAME:	HAIRY FROGFISH	SCIENTIFIC NAME:	ANTENNARIUS STRIATUS

SIZE:

9.8 INCHES
(25 CM)

WHERE THEY LIVE:

TROPICAL REGIONS OF THE ATLANTIC, PACIFIC, AND **INDIAN OCEANS** AND IN THE RED SEA

FASHION ICON
The hairy frogfish's body is covered in thousands of spines that look like—you guessed it—strands of hair! They give the fish a furry appearance quite unlike any other animal in the sea.

Imagine willing your **HAIR COLOR** to change on its own, no hair products needed. The frogfish does this, **COMPLETELY CHANGING ITS COLOR** over a few weeks to perfectly blend in with its environment. These animals can take on shades of **YELLOW, PINK, RED, BROWN, AND CREAM.**

IMPRESSIVE HEADGEAR
Frogfish have lures that they wave in front of their mouths like built-in fishing rods to attract prey. Some species' lures resemble shrimp, others look like worms, and still others pass for tiny squid.

MACARONI PENGUIN

COMMON NAME:	MACARONI PENGUIN	SCIENTIFIC NAME:	EUDYPTES CHRYSOLOPHUS

SIZE:

28 INCHES
(71 CM) TALL

WHERE THEY LIVE:

ANTARCTICA AND THE TIP OF SOUTH
AMERICA

MACARONI PENGUINS DON'T GROW THEIR COLORFUL CRESTS UNTIL ADULTHOOD.

WHAT'S IN A NAME?

When British explorers first spotted these unusual penguins in the 18th century, they named the birds after a fashion trend back home. "Macaronis" were men who wore showy clothes and extravagant wigs almost half their own height. We see the resemblance!

SHOWING OFF

Macaroni penguins use their crests to attract partners. During mating season, the penguins will bow forward, then stretch their beaks straight up, calling loudly and shaking their heads back and forth to call attention to their over-the-top hairdos.

For most birds, **BRIGHTLY COLORED PLUMAGE COMES FROM THE ANIMALS' DIET.** (Canaries, for example, get their sunny hue from yellow pigments in the seeds, fruits, and insects they eat.) But penguins are different. **THEIR COLORFUL TOPPERS COME FROM PIGMENTS THEY MAKE INSIDE THEIR BODIES.**

Both these animals sport impressive hair. The macaroni penguin has such a distinctive do that it helped inspire the animal's name. But when it comes to which critter is the true "hair" to the throne, it has to be the hairy frogfish. Not only can it change the color of its hairlike spines, but it actually uses this shaggy covering to help it catch prey. **THAT GIVES THE FROGFISH THE SUPERIOR STYLE!**

IN AN ANIMAL OLYMPICS,

which critters would be able to **HOIST MASSIVE WEIGHTS,** leap a great distance, or wrestle each other into submission? These two beasts face off in a battle to win the gold medal for **EARTH'S MOST POWERFUL ANIMAL.**

BROWN BEAR

> **A BROWN BEAR TROTS ALONG A RIVER,** flexing its massive shoulder muscles. At 800 pounds (363 kg), it weighs as much as a grand piano. Suddenly, the bear hears a noise and surges up on its powerful hind legs for a better look. Standing eight feet (2.4 m) tall, it towers over the ground. This animal is big, burly, and packed with power.

It takes a lot of food to fuel a brown bear's body. It will eat just about anything, from salmon to small mammals to berries, honey, and plants. In the fall, brown bears may chow down on as much as 90 pounds (40.8 kg) of food each day to prepare for hibernation. They lie low in their dens for most of winter. But even after months of inactivity their muscles remain superstrong.

BROWN BEAR
VS
★ ★
BENGAL TIGER

BENGAL TIGER

❯ **SOMETHING IS SLINKING THROUGH A RAINFOREST IN INDIA ...** something big. Nearly silent, it pads forward on giant paws, revealing a bold black-and-orange-striped coat. It's a Bengal tiger, one of the most dominant predators on Earth.

Bengal tigers are powerful predators that hunt in stealth mode. Their coats act as camouflage, allowing them to lie in wait without being seen until an animal such as a buffalo, deer, or wild pig wanders close. Then, the tiger pounces, using its strong muscles and sharp teeth and claws to take down its prey. As the largest members of the cat family and some of the toughest animals on Earth, Bengal tigers can conquer just about any other animal.

Stand back! These are some SERIOUS FEATS OF STRENGTH.

GRIZZLY BEARS, WHICH HAVE FUR TIPPED IN SILVER OR GRAY, ARE A **SUBSPECIES** OF BROWN BEAR.

IT'S PAW-SOME

A brown bear's massive paws sport five claws up to four inches (10.2 cm) long. Like built-in Swiss army knives, they're useful for all kinds of tasks, including digging dens in hard ground, ripping apart tree stumps to look for insects, and scooping up salmon from rivers.

Despite their enormous size, brown bears are **FAST**. With superstrong leg muscles to propel them forward, they've been clocked reaching **30 MILES AN HOUR (48 KM/H)**—fast enough to outrun a record-breaking human Olympic sprinter!

FEAT OF STRENGTH

In 2006, researchers at Montana State University, in Montana, U.S.A., tested the strength of brown bears. They found that the bears could roll a 700-pound (318-kg) metal Dumpster like it was a beach ball! Their conclusion: One bear is as strong as five humans put together.

BROWN BEAR

COMMON NAME:	BROWN BEAR	SCIENTIFIC NAME:	URSUS ARCTOS

SIZE:

UP TO **800** POUNDS (363 KG)

WHERE THEY LIVE:

THE FORESTS AND **MOUNTAINS** OF NORTHERN NORTH AMERICA, EUROPE, AND ASIA

BENGAL TIGER

| COMMON NAME: | BENGAL TIGER | SCIENTIFIC NAME: | PANTHERA TIGRIS TIGRIS |

SIZE:

UP TO
500 POUNDS
(227 KG)

WHERE THEY LIVE:

MAINLY IN
INDIA

A TIGER'S ROAR CAN BE HEARD AS FAR AS **TWO MILES** (3.2 KM) AWAY.

SHARP OBJECTS

A full-grown Bengal tiger is not a beast to be messed with. These enormous cats have up to four-inch (10-cm)-long claws, and paws so strong that a single swipe can smash a skull.

IT'S JAW-SOME

When you chow down on a tough bit of food, your jaw exerts a force of about 150 pounds per square inch (11 kg per sq cm). Compare that to a Bengal tiger's bite: It chomps down with about 1,000 pounds per square inch (70.3 kg per sq cm) of force!

Hunting takes a lot of energy. Though they usually eat much less, a **HUNGRY TIGER CAN CHOW DOWN ON AS MUCH AS 60 POUNDS (27 KG) IN A SINGLE NIGHT.** That's a fifth of its body weight, or the equivalent of a 10-year-old eating **28 HAMBURGERS IN ONE SITTING!**

We wouldn't want to go up against either of these mighty mammals. But when it comes to a competition for the most powerful, which creature is the winner? Both are strong, both are fast, and both are hungry. But while brown bears eat mostly foods like nuts, berries, and insects, along with the occasional small animal, Bengal tigers are fearsome hunters that regularly take down large prey.
TIGERS WIN BY A WHISKER!

EXTREME-LY
STRONG BUT TINY CRITTERS

NOT ALL OF EARTH'S MOST POWERFUL ANIMALS ARE MEGA SIZE.

These petite competitors might seem like lightweights, but pound for pound, THEY'RE SOME OF THE STRONGEST CRITTERS AROUND.

AFRICAN CROWNED EAGLE

African crowned eagles are perhaps the **MOST POWERFUL BIRDS ON THE PLANET.** They use their long hind talons to stage an attack, often dropping down from a tree onto an unsuspecting animal. Crowned eagles are able to **KILL ANIMALS WEIGHING UP TO 44 POUNDS (20 KG)**—more than four times their own size!

ASIAN WEAVER ANT

Weaver ants can effortlessly hold **100 TIMES THEIR BODY WEIGHT**—even while clinging upside down to a slick surface! The trick is in their special feet, which unfurl tiny pads that help the ants **STICK TO SMOOTH SURFACES, NO MATTER HOW HEAVY THE WEIGHT THEY'RE CARRYING.**

KING SNAKE
King snakes **KILL BY CONSTRICTING, OR WRAPPING, THEIR BODIES AROUND THEIR VICTIMS AND SQUEEZING THEM TO DEATH.** They are so strong that they can kill and **EAT SNAKES 20 PERCENT LARGER** than they are, squeezing them so hard they disrupt their foes' heartbeat and blood flow.

HONEY BADGER
This is one tough animal. Honey badgers are only about 10 inches (25 cm) tall, but they have **JAWS THAT CAN BREAK THROUGH A TURTLE SHELL,** paws that can dig a hiding place in minutes, and **SKIN SO THICK IT ACTS LIKE ARMOR** against stings and bites.

ORIBATID MITE
This critter is truly puny. **WEIGHING IN AT JUST A FRACTION OF AN OUNCE,** the oribatid mite is so small it's almost invisible in its home in the soil on the forest floor. But it is incredibly strong, able to **HOLD 1,180 TIMES ITS WEIGHT AND PULL 530 TIMES ITS WEIGHT.**

HORNED DUNG BEETLE
These beetles may spend most of their time **ROLLING BALLS OF POO**—but they are still one of Earth's most impressive creatures. The horned dung beetle can pull up to **1,141 TIMES ITS BODY WEIGHT**—the equivalent of a human dragging six double-decker buses!

CLOSEST BFFS

They may not SHARE POPCORN at the movies or BORROW EACH OTHER'S CLOTHES, but these animal BFFs have some of the

CLOSEST PARTNERSHIPS
IN NATURE.

CLOWNFISH AND ANEMONE

❯ A SEA ANEMONE WAVES ITS MULTICOLORED TENTACLES IN THE WATER. The creature is searching for prey: fish and whatever else wanders too close. At the slightest touch, the anemone's tentacles are triggered to inject a paralyzing toxin into its unsuspecting victim. But wait a minute ... between those toxic tentacles, a brightly colored clownfish is poking out its head!

Clownfish have a close relationship with certain species of anemones. The little fish live among the stinging sea creature's tentacles. Inside their toxic home, clownfish are protected from predators. In return for the shelter, they provide the anemone with food scraps from their meals, chase away intruders, and primp and preen their host to remove parasites. It's a marine match made in heaven!

MONGOOSE AND WARTHOG

❯ WARTHOGS SURE DON'T LOOK VERY FRIENDLY. These wild members of the pig family sport four sharp tusks and large heads covered with tufts of hair and wartlike bumps. They can weigh up to 250 pounds (113 kg) and run 30 miles an hour (48 km/h)—as fast as a charging bull! Yet, one group of warthogs has formed an unlikely partnership with a much smaller critter.

When warthogs at Queen Elizabeth National Park in Uganda spot a group of mongooses, they do something strange—they lie down! The mongooses surround the big pigs, climbing all over them and even jumping on their backs. Meanwhile, the warthogs lie there meekly. What's going on with this bizarre pairing?

CLOWNFISH & ANEMONE & VS MONGOOSE & WARTHOG

These animal friendships WILL MAKE YOU SAY *AWW!*

CLOWNFISH WILL SHARE THEIR ANEMONE HOME WITH OTHER CLOWNFISH WHEN **SPACE IS TIGHT.**

Most fish try to nibble on an anemone's tentacles, which prompts the **ANEMONE TO STRIKE.** But you won't find the clownfish snacking on the tentacles. It has evolved to avoid biting its buddy. **THAT'S ONLY POLITE!**

SLIME SHIELD
It's not easy living inside a home that stings. Some species of clownfish gently touch their host anemone again and again when they first move in. Scientists think this process adds chemicals to the natural layer of mucus the clownfish wear that tell the anemone not to sting.

SHARE THE AIR
Clownfish perform an intricate dance inside their anemone hosts, turning and weaving through their tentacles. Scientists recently discovered this dance isn't just for fun: It helps waft fresh, oxygen-rich water over the anemone so it can breathe.

WINNER

CLOWNFISH & ANEMONE

| COMMON NAME: | **CLOWNFISH & ANEMONE** | SCIENTIFIC NAME: | SUBFAMILY AMPHIPRIONINAE (CLOWNFISH) AND ORDER ACTINIARIA (ANEMONE) |

SIZE:

CLOWNFISH:
4.3 INCHES
(11 CM)

ANEMONE:
0.5 INCHES
(12.7 MM) TO 6 FEET (1.8 M)

WHERE THEY LIVE:
IN THE WARM WATERS OF THE
PACIFIC
AND INDIAN OCEANS

WARTHOG & MONGOOSE

COMMON NAME:	**WARTHOG & MONGOOSE**	SCIENTIFIC NAME:	**PHACOCHOERUS AFRICANUS (WARTHOG) FAMILY HERPESTIDAE (MONGOOSE)**

SIZE:

WHERE THEY LIVE:

WARTHOG:

120 to 250

POUNDS (54–113 KG)

MONGOOSE:

UP TO **11**

POUNDS (5 KG)

THE GRASSLANDS & SAVANNA WOODLANDS

OF **AFRICA***

*SOME MONGOOSES ALSO LIVE IN SPAIN AND PORTUGAL AND IN PARTS OF ASIA, WHERE THEY DON'T ENCOUNTER WARTHOGS.

PRIMPED PIG

When the warthog lies down, it's a signal to the mongoose that the bigger animal wants a spa treatment. The mongoose grooms the warthog, even cleaning inside its ears!

In exchange for their cleaning service, mongooses get a meal: **DEAD SKIN ALONG WITH TICKS AND OTHER PARASITES** are a tasty snack. As a thank-you, warthogs keep their tusks to themselves.

SECRET BUDS

Partnerships like this between mammals are almost unknown, say scientists. But this behavior made them wonder: Are there many more animal friendships like this in nature, just waiting to be discovered?

DESPITE THEIR APPEARANCE, WARTHOGS AREN'T FEROCIOUS: THEY ARE GRAZERS THAT **EAT GRASSES AND PLANTS.**

Which set of buddies is more attached? It's a close contest: Warthogs actually change their behavior to pair up with mongooses, lying down in the dirt and letting the furry critters hop right on them. (Normally, they do not transform into jungle gyms for other animals!) But a warthog and mongoose still aren't as tight as a clownfish and anemone twosome. This duo really depends on each other—in fact, **CLOWNFISH WOULD NOT BE ABLE TO SURVIVE WITHOUT THEIR ANEMONE PARTNERS. THAT MAKES THEM TRUE BFFS FOR LIFE!**

EXTREME-LY TIGHT ANIMAL PAIRS

THESE DYNAMIC DUOS BUDDY UP FOR THE BETTER.

OXPECKERS AND AFRICAN GRAZERS

There's more than meets the eye to this animal partnership. It's often said that oxpecker birds ride on the backs of rhinos, zebras, giraffes, and antelopes, **PICKING OFF ANNOYING TICKS** while the big animals munch on grass. The grazers get **PARASITE PATROL**, and the birds get a meal. But the oxpecker isn't just a helper—it's also a parasite that snacks on the **BLOOD OF ITS HOSTS.** Relationship status: It's complicated.

CARRION BEETLES AND MITES

Carrion beetles have a lifestyle some might find unpleasant: **THEY EAT THE ROTTING CARCASSES OF DEAD ANIMALS,** also called carrion. Even grosser, they lay their eggs on the carcasses to ensure their young have a meal when they hatch. But other insects have discovered the same trick, meaning there's lots of competition. So the beetles have developed a surprising strategy: **THEY CARRY MITES ON THEIR BACKS TO EACH NEW CARCASS.** The mites eat the eggs of other insects, leaving only the beetle eggs. The beetle babies get a jump start in life, and the mites get a meal.

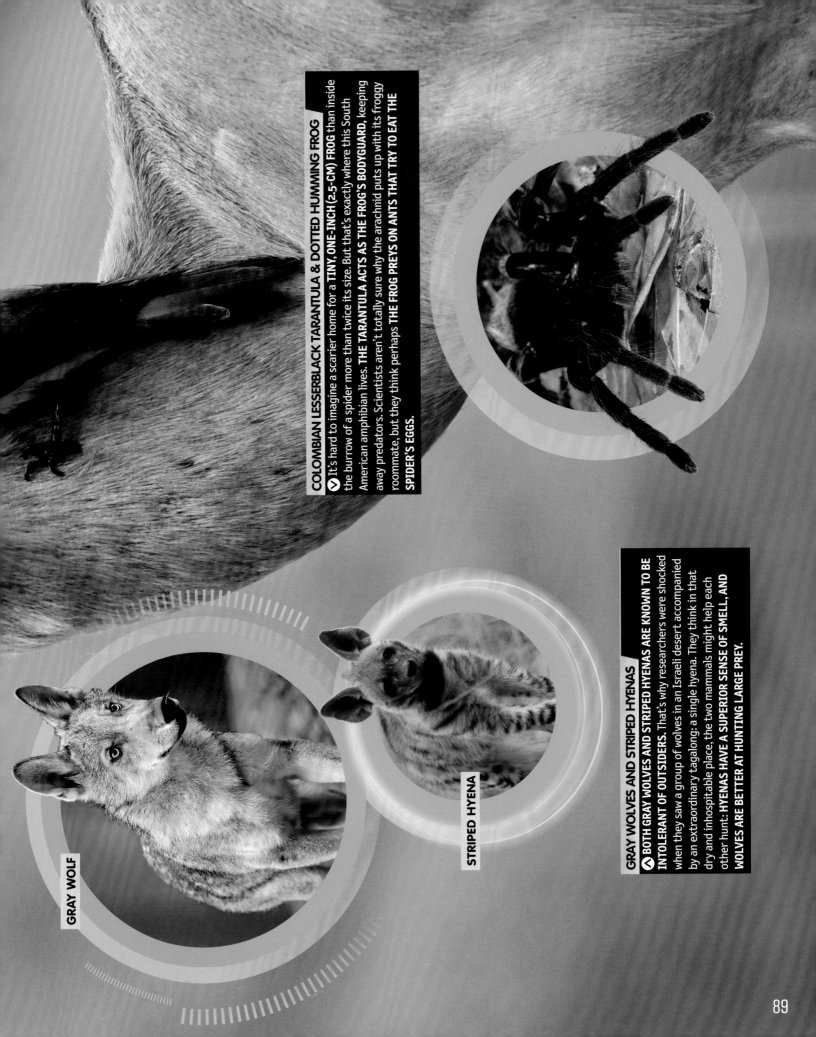

COLOMBIAN LESSERBLACK TARANTULA & DOTTED HUMMING FROG

It's hard to imagine a scarier home for a **TINY, ONE-INCH (2.5-CM) FROG** than inside the burrow of a spider more than twice its size. But that's exactly where this South American amphibian lives. **THE TARANTULA ACTS AS THE FROG'S BODYGUARD,** keeping away predators. Scientists aren't totally sure why the arachnid puts up with its froggy roommate, but they think perhaps **THE FROG PREYS ON ANTS THAT TRY TO EAT THE SPIDER'S EGGS.**

GRAY WOLVES AND STRIPED HYENAS

BOTH GRAY WOLVES AND STRIPED HYENAS ARE KNOWN TO BE INTOLERANT OF OUTSIDERS. That's why researchers were shocked when they saw a group of wolves in an Israeli desert accompanied by an extraordinary tagalong: a single hyena. They think in that dry and inhospitable place, the two mammals might help each other hunt: **HYENAS HAVE A SUPERIOR SENSE OF SMELL, AND WOLVES ARE BETTER AT HUNTING LARGE PREY.**

GRAY WOLF

STRIPED HYENA

ANIMAL EATING CONTEST

Think you've got a **BIG APPETITE?** These hungry critters can *REALLY PACK IT AWAY.* In terms of pure poundage, some might not seem so impressive … but compared to their body size, their

MEALS ARE MASSIVE!

ASIAN ELEPHANT

NEARLY
800
POUNDS
(363 KG) PER DAY
OR
10%
OF BODY WEIGHT

.003
POUNDS
(.001 KG) PER DAY OR
100%
OF BODY WEIGHT

MONARCH CATERPILLAR

BLUE WHALE

8,000
POUNDS
(3,629 KG) PER DAY
OR
2%
OF BODY WEIGHT

28
POUNDS
(12.7 KG) PER DAY
OR
12%
OF BODY WEIGHT

.012
POUNDS
(.005 KG) PER DAY
OR
200%
OF BODY WEIGHT

RUBY-THROATED
HUMMINGBIRD

.01
POUNDS
(.004 KG) PER DAY
OR
125%
OF BODY WEIGHT

WINNER

GIANT PANDA

PYGMY SHREW

INDEX

CREDITS

Cover: (chameleon), Claude Thouvenin/Biosphoto; (cuttlefish), Gabriel Barathieu/Biosphoto; (LO RT), apple2499/Shutterstock; (LO LE), Floriana/Adobe Stock; (jellyfish), Channarong Sae-Tang/Shutterstock; (scorpion), Stephen Dalton/Science Source; **back cover:** (woodchuck), vasin/Adobe Stock; (crocodile), Stu Porter/Shutterstock; (fish), Alex Mustard/Nature Picture Library; (penguin), Marco Simoni/Getty Images; (fisher), Wayne Lynch/All Canada Photos/Alamy Stock Photo; (wolverine), tbkmedia.de/Alamy Stock Photo; 4 (UP RT), Daniel Prudek/Shutterstock; 4 (LO RT), Thomas Marent/Minden Pictures; 4 (LO LE), Michael Lynch/Shutterstock; 5 (UP LE), Melinda Fawver/Shutterstock; 5 (UP CTR), Ann and Steve Toon/NPL/Minden Pictures; 5 (UP RT), Daniel Heuclin/NPL/Minden Pictures; 5 (CTR), Marco Simoni/Getty Images; 5 (LO), Steve Bloom Images/Alamy Stock Photo; 6 (UP LE), Arnaud Weisser/Shutterstock; 6 (UP RT), Steve Bloom Images/Alamy Stock Photo; 6 (LO RT), Kelvin Aitken/Biosphoto; 6 (LO LE), Palex66/Dreamstime; 7 (CTR LE), Petershort/Getty Images; 7 (UP RT), TheBladler/Getty Images; 7 (CTR RT), Glenn Bartley/age fotostock; 7 (LO), MYN/Lily Kumpe/Minden Pictures; 8, tbkmedia.de/Alamy Stock Photo; 9, Cathy & Gordon Illg/Jaynes Gallery/Danita Delimont/Danita Delimont.com; 10 (LE), Dieter Hopf/imageBROKER/Shutterstock; 10 (CTR), Christophe Perelle/Biosphoto; 10 (RT), Popova Valeriya/Shutterstock; 10 (UP RT), Juan Carlos Muñoz/age fotostock; 10 (LO RT), Arterra Picture Library/Alamy Stock Photo; 11 (UP LE), Andy Sands/NPL/Minden Pictures; 11 (LO LE), Robert Dziewulski/Shutterstock; 11 (LE), Eric Isselee/Shutterstock; 11 (CTR), Eric Isselee/Shutterstock; 11 (RT), GlobalP/iStock/Getty Images; 12-13, Holger Ehlers/Alamy Stock Photo; 12, Razvan Ciuca/Getty Images; 13 (UP LE), Nature Picture Library/Alamy Stock Photo; 13 (UP RT), Sren Pedersen/EyeEm/Getty Images; 13 (LO RT), ShaftInAction/iStock/Getty Images; 13 (LO LE), Secret Sea Visions/Getty Images; 14, Glenn Bartley/BIA/Minden Pictures; 15, Doug Perrine/NPL/Minden Pictures; 16 (LE), Mike Truchon/Shutterstock; 16 (CTR), RooM the Agency/Alamy Stock Photo; 16 (RT), Aniko Gerendi Enderle/Shutterstock; 16 (UP RT), Backyardphotography707/Dreamstime; 16 (LO RT), David G Hemmings/Getty Images; 17 (UP LE), Jody Watt/Getty Images; 17 (CTR LE), Duncan Murrell/Alamy Stock Photo; 17 (LE), M Swiet Productions/Moment/Getty Images; 17 (CTR), TheBladler/Getty Images; 17 (RT), PaulVinten/iStock/Getty Images; 18-19, Scott Linstead/Science Source; 18 (LE), Dominic Robinson/Alamy Stock Photo; 18 (RT), dean bertoncelj/Shutterstock; 19 (UP), Philip Dalton/Alamy Stock Photo; 19 (RT), Santiago mc/Getty Images; 19 (LE), Paul S. Wolf/Shutterstock; 20, Mark Bowler/Science Source/Getty Images; 21, Mathieu Meur/Stocktrek Images/Getty Images; 22 (LE), jaana piira/Shutterstock; 22 (CTR), Ana Francisconi/EyeEm/Getty Images; 22 (RT), Michael Nolan/robertharding/Alamy Stock Images; 22 (UP RT), jocrebbin/iStock/Getty Images; 22 (LO RT), Education Images/Getty Images; 23 (UP LE), J W Alker/imageBROKER/Shutterstock; 23 (CTR LE), WaterFrame/Alamy Stock Photo; 23 (LE), Dana.S/Shutterstock; 23 (CTR), Helmut Corneli/Alamy Stock Photo; 23 (RT), Colin Marshall/Minden Pictures; 24-25, Reinhard Mink/Getty Images; 24 (LE), Fran Hall/Science Source; 24 (RT), ANP PHhoto/age fotostock; 25 (CTR RT), Dr. Natasha Mhatre; 25 (CTR), Thomas Marent/Minden Pictures; 25 (LO RT), Thomas Marent/Minden Pictures; 26, imageBROKER/Josef Niedermeier/Biosphoto; 27, Tobias Bernhard Raff/Biosphoto/Minden Pictures; 28 (LE), Gary Davis/EyeEm/Getty Images; 28 (CTR), Arnaud Weisser/Shutterstock; 28 (RT), Mark Bridger/Getty Images; 28 (UP RT), Dissoid/Getty Images; 28 (LO RT), C. K. Lorenz/Science Source; 29 (UP LE), Alan James/NPL/Minden Pictures; 29 (LO LE), Dray van Beeck/NiS/Minden Pictures; 29 (LE), Matthias Graben/Getty Images; 29 (CTR), imageBROKER/SeaTops/Biosphoto; 29 (RT), Georgette Douwma/NPL/Minden Pictures; 30-31, Cathy Keifer/Dreamstime; 30 (UP), Andrew Snyder/NPL/Minden Pictures; 30 (LO), Westbury/Getty Images; 31 (UP LE), dikkyoesin1/Getty Images; 31 (UP RT), StÈphan Bonneau/Biosphoto; 31 (LO RT), Brandon Cole/Biosphoto; 32, Michael Lynch/Shutterstock; 33, Thomas Marent/Minden Pictures; 34 (LE), Geerati Nilkaew/Alamy Stock Photo; 34 (CTR), Jens Rydell/Johner RF/Getty Images; 34 (RT), Barry Mansell/Minden Pictures; 34 (UP RT), Stephen Dalton/NHPA/Photoshot; 34 (LO RT), Steve Bloom Images/Alamy Stock Photo; 35 (UP LE), Arco Images GmbH/Alamy Stock Photo; 35 (LO LE), BIOSPHOTO/Alamy Stock Photo; 35 (LE), John Abbott/Minden Pictures; 35 (CTR), Piotr Naskrecki/Minden Pictures; 35 (RT), MYN/Andrew Snyder/NPL/Minden Pictures; 36-37, Thorsten Negro/Getty Images; 36, Steve Downer/Science Source; 37 (UP LE), NatalieJean/Shutterstock; 37 (UP RT), Pete Oxford/Danita Delimont.com; 37 (CTR RT), Julie DeRoche/Design Pics/Getty Images; 37 (LO RT), Oliver Thompson-Holmes/Alamy Stock Photo; 38, Pascal Kobeh/Minden Pictures; 39, Joseph Tepper; 40 (LE), Douglas Streakley/Lonely Planet Images/Getty Images; 40 (CTR), blickwinkel/Alamy Stock Photo; 40 (RT), Doug Perrine/Alamy Stock Photo; 40 (UP RT), phonlamaiphoto/Dreamstime; 40 (CTR RT), Pascal Kobeh/Minden Pictures; 41 (UP LE), Jennifer Hayes/National Geographic Creative; 41 (LO LE), Todd Pusser/Nature Picture Library; 41 (LE), Todd Pusser/Nature Picture Library; 41 (CTR), Joseph Tepper; 41 (RT), Todd Pusser/Nature Picture Library; 42, Stephen Dalton/Science Source; 43, Melanie Stetson Freeman/Getty Images; 44 (LE), Daniel Heuclin/NPL/Minden Pictures; 44 (CTR), IMAGEMORE/Getty Images; 44 (RT), Palex66/Dreamstime; 44 (UP RT), Laguna Design/Science Source; 44 (CTR RT), Protasov AN/Shutterstock; 45 (UP LE), Paul Sutherland/National Geographic Image Collection; 45 (LO LE), Dennis Kunkel Microscopy/Science Source; 45 (LE), Kelvin Aitken/Biosphoto; 45 (CTR), Ben & Lynn Cropp/AUSCAPE/Getty Images; 45 (RT), Karen Gowlett-Holmes/Getty Images; 46-47, Anna Kucherova/Shutterstock; 46 (LE), Morley Read/Getty Images; 46 (RT), Daniel Heuclin/Science Source; 47 (UP RT), Dave Watts/Biosphoto; 47 (CTR RT), vovashevchuk/iStockphoto/Getty Images; 47 (LO LE), Eloi_Omella/iStockphoto/Getty Images; 48, Anup Shah/Minden Pictures; 49, Riccardo Oggioni/Alamy Stock Photo; 50 (LE), Anton Petrus/Getty Images; 50 (CTR), Jami Tarris/Getty Images; 50 (RT), Bennie Moore/EyeEm/Getty Images; 50 (UP RT), Anup Shah/NPL/Minden Pictures; 50 (LO RT), Romeo Gacad/AFP/Getty Images; 51 (UP LE), Albert Lleal/Minden Pictures; 51 (CTR LE), Konrad Wothe/Minden Pictures; 51 (LE), Dirk Ercken/Shutterstock; 51 (CTR), Thomas Marent/Minden Pictures; 51 (RT), Dirk Ercken/Shutterstock; 52, NPS Photo/Alamy Stock Photo; 53, Scott Leslie/Minden Pictures; 54 (LE), Martha Holmes/Nature Picture Library; 54 (CTR), Paul Nicklen/National Geographic Image Collection; 54 (RT), Nature Picture Library/Alamy Stock Photo; 54 (UP

For Aunt Gina, who loves both the beautiful and the bizarre —SWD

Since 1888, the National Geographic Society has funded more than 12,000 research, exploration, and preservation projects around the world. The Society receives funds from National Geographic Partners, LLC, funded in part by your purchase. A portion of the proceeds from this book supports this vital work. To learn more, visit natgeo.com/info.

For more information, visit nationalgeographic.com, call 1-877-873-6846, or write to the following address:

National Geographic Partners
1145 17th Street N.W.
Washington, D.C. 20036-4688 U.S.A.

Visit us online at nationalgeographic.com/books

For librarians and teachers: nationalgeographic.com/books /librarians-and-educators

More for kids from National Geographic: natgeokids.com

National Geographic Kids magazine inspires children to explore their world with fun yet educational articles on animals, science, nature, and more. Using fresh storytelling and amazing photography, *Nat Geo Kids* shows kids ages 6 to 14 the fascinating truth about the world—and why they should care. **kids.nationalgeographic.com/subscribe**

For rights or permissions inquiries, please contact National Geographic Books Subsidiary Rights: bookrights@natgeo.com

Designed by Fuszion Collaborative, Inc.

Library of Congress Cataloging-in-Publication Data

Names: Drimmer, Stephanie Warren, author.
Title: Animal showdown : round three/by Stephanie Warren Drimmer.
Description: Washington, DC : National Geographic Kids, 2020. | Series: Animal showdown | Audience: Ages 8-12 | Audience: Grades 4-6 | Summary: "Information about different animals and how they would match up, for children"-- Provided by publisher.
Identifiers: LCCN 2019036375 | ISBN 9781426338427 (paperback) | ISBN 9781426338434 (library binding)
Subjects: LCSH: Animals--Juvenile literature.
Classification: LCC QL49 .D755 2020 | DDC 590--dc23
LC record available at https://lccn.loc.gov/2019036375

The publisher would like to thank everyone who helped make this book possible: Shelby Lees, senior editor; Andrea Silen, text editor; Brett Challos, art director; Shannon Hibberd, senior photo editor; Marti Davila and Rick Heffner at Fuszion; Liz Seramur, freelance photo editor; Molly Reid, production editor; Robin Palmer, fact-checker; and Gus Tello and Anne LeongSon, design production assistants.

Printed in China
20/RRDH/1